Hot Dogs On The Road

Hot Dogs On The Road

An American Indian girl's reflections on growing
up brown in a black and white world

LENA EPPS BROOKER

In loving memory of my parents,
Frank Howard Epps and Grace Smith Epps.

With love, they gave me life and taught me how to live.

Acknowledgments

To Jim Brooker, my husband, for your love and patience.
To Cam Epps, my "baby brother," for sharing memories.
To Jackie Potter, my editor, for your expertise.
To Gloria Lowery, my friend, for the beautiful cover art.

And Franklin Epps, my brother in heaven, for his encouragement while on earth.

Together, we made it happen with God as our guide.

Contents

Reasons

The Way to Here

North Carolina is home to the largest population of Native Americans east of the Mississippi River, yet few outside the borders of my birth county (Robeson) and those counties with significant Indian populations know this. People have a general awareness of the Cherokee Nation, located in western North Carolina, but they have little knowledge of the presence of Lumbee Indians—the largest of the American Indian groups—or the other state-recognized tribes and organizations found across the Tar Heel State.

It will come as no surprise, then, that the realities of life for American Indians in North Carolina are still little known. This is especially true for the time period when I was a young girl growing up in the Saddletree community of Robeson County in the '40s and '50s. History books have barely noted our existence over the years and have rarely addressed our lives in any way. My people were largely lost between the cracks of a black and white society.

What I discovered once I lived outside Robeson County was that the majority of people I met understood neither the blessings nor the burdens of being an American Indian. Without fully realizing it, I found myself facing color barriers and also educating people about the realities of life for those of us who were the First People here. Classrooms, places of work and worship, neighborhood socials, boardrooms, town councils, community organizations, political gatherings, and presidential commissions have all heard parts of my story of being an American Indian in a mostly white and black world. This became a large part of "The Way" I lived and who I was.

The Way to live is critical to most American Indian people. It defines goals, attitudes, actions, and, ultimately, the quality of life not only for the individual but also for the community. The Way, as I learned it from my parents, involves respect and reverence for God, the Creator of everything. It also includes the recognition that no human being is superior to another and that what we do to any part of Creation, we also do to ourselves. While not traditional according to some Indian views of the time (or even now), it was the "right way" and the "best way" because my parents believed it was God's way. At the time I was growing up, it was the best way because it was Mama and Daddy's way.

A fundamental piece of the Way that I inherited from my parents is this: *there is often more to life than meets the eye.* I share these stories to acknowledge the many people who know all too well what it really means to be a brown American Indian in a black and white world.

The Way to here has been both long and short. Some moments and experiences were never long enough; sometimes, moments and events lasted far too long. Along the way I have laughed loudly, wept bitterly, questioned often, and loved fiercely. In recent years I have learned to express outrage, exclaim awe, and live with gratitude as a constant companion. Each experience, whether I considered it a blessing or a burden, taught me more about the Way to live. Sometimes I learned what to do or how to be; other times I learned what to avoid or when to denounce. My way to here is a journey I would not trade.

Read these stories with your eyes and listen with your heart. They are meant to honor all my people; their journey was never easy, but they continued to believe that being American Indian was one of life's best blessings. If others learn more about American Indians in North Carolina as a result of my reflections, then that would be the reward for sharing part of my life's journey on the way to here.

Reasons-Locations

Rare Ones

Beginnings

My life started long before I was born. The births in North Carolina of Frank Howard Epps in 1904 in the High Plains community of Person County and of Grace Evelyn Smith in 1915 in the Saddletree community of Robeson County were my beginnings.

Though they didn't meet, fall in love, and marry until many years later, they held several individual experiences in common. Both were the first born in their families, and both participated in providing care to younger siblings. Changing a baby's diaper was nothing new, chasing toddlers away from unsuitable places to play a familiar task, and getting little ones dressed an assignment they performed routinely. They witnessed heartache at its worst when both saw their parents grieve over a young child who had died. And they learned early and better than many adults that children demanded constant care and resources. More than anything, they saw and experienced the faith, hope, and love of their parents.

They worked in farm fields and knew the smell of sweat, the feelings of exhaustion, and the desire to get to sleep at an early hour. Each knew the predictable routine that would follow the next day when farming was in season. They recognized their parents' struggles to earn a living and at the same time encourage their children to get as much education as possible. Miles apart and unknown in any way to the other, each decided to pursue a dream: they dreamed of graduating from college.

Rev. D.F. Lowry, an American Indian Methodist minister and schoolteacher from Pembroke, North Carolina, learned that the Person County Indians had no opportunities for high school at the time, so he visited the High Plains community and arranged for Frank to live with his family and complete high school in Pembroke. Rev. Lowry then assisted him in receiving a work-study scholarship to McKendree College, a small Methodist-supported school in Lebanon, Illinois. This oldest child of Zan and Mary Martin Epps became the first in his community to graduate from college. He felt a deep and lifelong gratitude for the role Rev. Lowry had played in his life. Following his graduation in 1931, Frank Epps taught at the school for American Indians in Sampson County, North Carolina, for two years. In 1933 he accepted the position of principal at Magnolia School in the Saddletree community of Robeson County and boarded with the family of the Rev. S. A. Hammonds, whose home was in the same community.

The family of Grace Evelyn Smith moved from Saddletree to the Prospect community when she was very young and later to Pembroke, where she graduated from the Indian high school. She then graduated from the Indian Normal School in Pembroke, a state-supported two-year program that trained American Indians to become teachers. In 1935 Grace began her career in education at Barker Ten Mile School and lived with her aunt Ellen Smith Carter and family. She and Miss Magdalene Chavis, a woman who also taught at the same school and became a lifelong friend, often walked more than two miles to reach the wooden school that served the Indians in the Antioch community, a few miles from the small town of St. Pauls.

Grace Evelyn Smith's family attended the First Methodist Church in Pembroke, as did Rev. Lowry and his family. On many weekends, she returned to visit with her family in Pembroke, and Frank Howard Epps returned to spend weekends with Rev. Lowry and his family. While the

Smith and Lowry families lived near each other, attending church was likely where a connection began that eventually blossomed and bloomed into romance and then love between young Grace Smith and Frank Epps, who was eleven years older than Grace. Henry Smith, Grace's youngest brother, retold stories of the bachelor from Person County coming to court his sister Grace on a motor scooter. Henry told how he would ask for rides and often was allowed to do so. When Frank, the suitor, was reluctant, Henry said he resorted to twenty-five-cent bribes, or he would threaten to tell his mother, Lela Locklear Smith, that Frank and Grace had been sitting too close on the sofa.

In November of 1937, the marriage of Frank Howard Epps and Grace Evelyn Smith occurred at the home of the Rev. and Mrs. S. A. Hammonds Sr., in the heart of Saddletree. It was Thanksgiving, a splendid day for the beginning of a new life together, which was always characterized by their love for each other and their families, their commitment and service to American Indian people, and, above all, their faith in God.

The young couple rented a house and adjoining farmland off Rennert Road, a short distance from the home of the Hammonds family. To assist with farming duties, Zan Jr. and Alfred Epps, brothers of the new groom, traveled from Person County and lived with the newlyweds. Money was limited, and meals were meager.

"Pass that fried chicken around, Grace," Frank said to his bride. "And don't forget the rice and gravy."

A plate piled with fried fatback made its way around the table, followed by a plate of biscuits covered with molasses—if they had any. Their first home was a structure constructed of untreated, unpainted lumber with an outside toilet and no running water.

Each intimately learned about adversity and hope, and together they experienced some of the blessings and burdens of life. Because the Saddletree community had no Indian Methodist church, and Mrs. Sarah Margaret Hammonds, the wife of the Rev. S. A. Hammonds, attended Ten Mile Center Baptist Church (near the Magnolia School), the young couple worshipped regularly there. I, as yet unknown and unborn to them, lived blissfully in the "Mystical Sea." According to my grandmother Lela Smith, that's where all babies lived until they were born.

It was to these two American Indians—Frank Howard Epps, a quiet, gentle man with a shy smile, and Grace Evelyn Smith, a lively, lovely, talkative woman—that I was born. Those who knew them well say that my dad longed for a baby girl. They also tell me that my parents rejoiced at my birth. My parents showered me with affection and guidance, as did our relatives and other people in our community. I was "Miss" Grace's and Mr. Epps's little girl to many people. (We called all women "Miss" whether they were single or married.) But by the time I was four years old, I considered myself Daddy's little girl. My mother recognized this special bond between the two of us and made room in her heart for our daddy-daughter relationship to grow. It did so with few words but with many smiles and pats on the head.

Shortly after I turned four, my brother Franklin was born, and sixteen months later my brother Cameron arrived. Though our family dynamics changed many times over the years, two things remained the same. First, we were surrounded by pure and simple love from the beginning. No matter what we did or what others did to us, we were loved. We were not just children; we were *their* children. We were loved because we were of their blood. And on this earth, to them, there was no greater love.

Intertwined tightly with their love for us was another constant. Daddy and Mama always held high hopes for the future of their children. They believed that we should and could have a life of promise. From our earliest days, they never faltered in that belief, though they knew that the barriers they had faced as children living in a tri-racially segregated society would confront us as well. They wanted new options for their children, starting with acceptance of our American Indian heritage as a blessing, not a burden.

Both my parents believed that education was the key to a better life for all people, but especially our people, American Indians. Not only would we fare better economically, they taught us, but we and people from different racial and ethnic backgrounds could also live together, with more openness and acceptance, with educated minds. It was this belief that kept them in the educational system of Robeson County, though it would have been far easier to work elsewhere.

The value of education motivated my parents to increase their personal education. My mother received her bachelor of arts degree at Pembroke State College in June 1942, not quite a year after I was born. She was the first in her family to do so. In the early fifties, my father enrolled in a master's degree program at Appalachian State University, the only North Carolina graduate school that would allow him to do so. He commuted to Boone, a 500 mile roundtrip from home, on weekends during the school year to attend classes. He usually rode a bus through numerous small towns and winding, two-lane mountain roads on Friday afternoons and returned on late Sunday afternoon. His principal duties began before eight the next morning.

At my father's suggestion and with his full support, my mother enrolled in a similar graduate program at Appalachian. One semester she lived in Boone and took me with her while my dad and his sister, Lois Epps Jones, cared for my brothers and Lois's son Larry at our home. The summer of 1952 was when my parents took their last graduate school classes at Appalachian, and our entire family spent the summer months in Boone. My dad rented a furnished house with a large yard that bordered a pasture with horses and cherry trees inside its wooden rail fences. The horses probably never recovered from my little brothers' antics. Without question, the cherry crop the pasture's owner harvested was slim.

At summer's end, I was tired of chasing my brothers, refereeing disagreements, and making sandwiches for lunch. But I was old enough to understand the significance of Mama and Daddy receiving their master's degrees and was happy for them. It was fun trying to locate our parents among the many people with black caps and gowns. Someone gave a boring speech that my brothers and I didn't hear. And Grandmother

Lela's efforts to keep my brothers and me from giggling every time we heard the words "summa cum laude" were unsuccessful.

Love, hope, and education were necessary for the best possible life here on earth, according to my parents. But faith was the foundation for every important undertaking in their lives—including their work as educators—and was the basis for their involvement in church activities and civic organizations. Often, they were the only Indian people in civic and community groups. People sometimes praised them for breaking race and color barriers. At other times they were denounced. Undeterred by either, they served because they believed it was an opportunity to help our people and others. After all, all people were God's people.

Daddy and Mama were certain that faith, love, and service were the beginnings of a later life that would be eternal. The lives of their three children began and continued with their faith, hope, and love. Mama and Daddy believed it was the least they could do (and also the most they could do) for their children. Thousands of other Indian children benefitted as well.

What I know with great certainty is this: what they gave me was more than enough to make all my beginnings bright, both in the past and now.

Rare Ones-Photographs

Frank Howard Epps- *a student at McKendree College around 1929 or 1930.*

*Grace Evelyn Smith -gave this photograph to Frank Howard
Epps sometime before their marriage in 1937.*

Innocence

Rides across the River

*G*oing to town was something I didn't do often when I was very young. My family lived in the rural community of Saddletree in Robeson County where pine trees grew tall and the soil beneath our bare feet lay dark and rich. Seven miles to the south of us was the county seat of Lumberton, and seven miles to the north was the small town of St Pauls. Highway 301 was the busy link to both, but a little brown Indian girl had few reasons to visit either.

The main reason for me to go to Lumberton was a need, not a diversion. My mother took me to town to buy clothes and shoes, and most often we shopped at either Belk's or Penney's. In the late summer, she and I went to town to buy a few new school clothes. A trip in May meant a school-closing outfit. But the highlight of those shopping ventures was seeing the absolutely unbelievable X-ray image of my foot in the shoe-sizing machine at Belk's Department Store. It was magic, pure and simple!

Looking down on a screen in the machine, I could clearly see every bone in my foot. In spite of the image's sickly green color, I could tell how much room there was between my toes and the end of the shoes.

According to Mama, that was the most important factor in buying a new pair of shoes.

"Don't leave your foot in there too long, or it'll turn green," I'd heard mothers tell their children on numerous occasions. Even one of my friends said, "You know, Evelena, you can catch a foot disease that'll spread all over your body if you leave your foot in that machine for too long. That's what my aunt told me."

I never really believed those stories about what could happen to my foot or body if I left my foot in this magic machine longer than necessary, but I didn't risk suffering unspeakable foot or body changes, either. When the sales clerk said she'd determined what shoe size I needed, my foot quickly came out of the contraption that could see straight through my skin to my bones.

Buying dresses was neither as simple nor as exciting as the foot-sizing machine. There was the issue of agreement on the colors and patterns of the dresses. My mother favored subdued colors and small patterns with a white collar, while I usually fell in love with a dress that had bright colors and bold patterns. The usual compromise was that the bright and bold dresses I got were for school, and a Sunday dress was one that my mother liked.

Prior to my entering the fourth grade, my mother could look at a dress and tell if it were the correct size. As I started getting taller and thinner, however, she insisted that I try the dresses on in the store's dressing room. And that caused me to be somewhat apprehensive.

Two of my classmates had shared some disturbing news with me. They said that Indians were not allowed to use the dressing rooms at Belk's or Penney's. They explained that if one's skin was light enough to be mistaken for that of a white person, then it didn't matter. But dark-skinned Indians were forbidden to try on clothes. I didn't believe that, but when the time came for me to try on the dresses, I tried to talk my mother into just buying them.

Of course, my mother insisted that I try on the dresses, and she also insisted that I come out of the dressing room so she could see me in them. As I turned for her to inspect the fit of the dress, I tried to be very casual about looking to find where the clerks were. None of them approached us, and I was very glad. I wasn't sure what would have happened had they come our way, but I was glad I didn't have to find out.

With a new dress or two and a new pair of shoes, my town business was completed. Mama led the way back to the car, which was often parked near Penney's. Leaving the parking lot, we often made a loop from the east end of downtown, drove over the Fifth Street Bridge, and then crossed the Second Street Bridge on our way home. This was not the most direct route home, but it kept Mama from making left turns in front of downtown traffic. It kept her calmer, but it made me tense.

The Fifth Street Bridge had concrete retaining walls that were fairly tall. If I stretched my neck and raised my body a bit off the car seat, I could see the dark waters of the Lumber River. But the truth was that I really didn't want to see the waters of the Lumber River. I was afraid of what I might see.

As we crossed the bridge, images of snakes were ever present in my mind. I remembered the stories Mr. Tom Burnette, a family friend, told about the Lumber River and the wildlife in and around it. One story that struck terror in my heart was about snakes falling out of the trees that overhung the river. Mr. Tom said that some of the snakes were so big and strong that some poor souls, whose boats the snakes fell into, were strangled to death by the tree snakes.

That was a nightmare that made me shiver. I didn't want to believe I'd see a snake as we crossed the river. But just to make sure, I didn't look down at the river either. The quicker we exited the bridge, the happier I'd be—except that now we approached the Robeson County Jail. This place wasn't any more pleasant than the bridge, I thought. I'd never heard about strangling snakes in the jailhouse, but people said some awful things about the place. People were locked up for terrible murders, and that was a good thing. People said that, as part of the prisoners' punishment, the jailers tried to starve them to death. When I asked the older students at school how they did this, my older classmates said the prisoners were fed one slice of bread and one cup of water each day. Not one other thing!

But that didn't compare to the real horror I'd heard about the jail. According to my school-yard sources, some of the men in jail were waiting to be "fried" in the electric chair. The image of someone being fried like fatback on Mama's stove was more than I could handle. But still I wondered: Did they sizzle and shrink like fatback? Did they turn brown as they fried? And, worst of all, did they scream as they cooked? I tried to clear those thoughts from my head by thinking about what I'd tell Franklin and Cam about my trip to town with Mama.

My little brothers wouldn't care about the new clothes and the pair of shoes I got in town, but I was certain they'd be sorry they'd missed the shoe-sizing machine. What would really make them sit, listen, and envy me would be the details of all the strange sights I saw while crossing the river on the Second Street Bridge. I couldn't wait to tell them about the huge, dark snake hanging from the tree, waiting to fall into the next small boat that came that way. Franklin and Cam would really wish they'd been with me for that ride across the river.

On many Saturday mornings, one of my parents went to town to buy groceries, conduct business at the bank, or do other errands. I understood at a very early age that they could manage town business without the benefit of my help or that of my brothers. Franklin, Cam and I did what country children were supposed to do on Saturdays: perform chores, play alone or with each other, and torment one another endlessly.

On the rare Saturday morning when my dad asked if I'd like to "ride to town" with him, I felt especially lucky. Time alone with my dad was always special, but a trip to town with him was an extraordinary treat. The places we went varied and were dictated mostly by the season of the year, because my educator dad was also a farmer. We often went to the Lumberton Trading Company, a large farm-supply store, or sometimes we stopped at the FCX store, where Daddy purchased seeds for crops yet to be planted. My favorite was a visit to the Scottish Bank, where a portrait of the corporate logo, Sagacious McThrift, greeted us from his lofty perch on the wall.

Something about the Scottish Bank was different from the other places we went on our Saturday visits to town. I couldn't tell you at the time what it was, but I could tell you how it felt. The bank employees seemed to respond to my dad, and to me, with a friendlier attitude than other business establishments did. He was greeted with a smile, and I remember some people who "waited on us" called him Professor Epps. Mrs. Clark, the employee who most often handled whatever transaction my dad made, was always gracious and smiled warmly. She addressed my dad as Mr. Epps. I was too young to know why Daddy was called both Professor Epps and Mr. Epps. I didn't know that "professor" was a term that gave some respect to nonwhite men but not the full respect of "mister," which was reserved for white men of my father's age and educational status.

Actually, what really mattered the most to me in the bank was whether some kind and generous person would give me a couple of pennies to insert into the floor-model bubble gum machine that stood against one of the tall interior pillars of that very formal institution. I would chew that bubble gum to death before my brothers ever heard about its existence. This was a big reward of a ride into town with my dad.

No matter what our itinerary, we never talked much, for my dad was a quiet man. At that time, I was my father's child in that respect. I liked to watch and listen as Daddy took care of his business. But most of the time, I looked at the people I saw—and there were plenty of people to see in town on Saturday. I saw black and brown people—some of whom could have belonged to either group and a few white people. It seemed that most of the white people I saw were working, not shopping.

Some people of all colors, but especially black and brown people, walked up and down the streets, lounged on the backs of cars, or talked in small groups on the sidewalks. One common sight on Saturdays was a man from our community sitting on an iron bench on the southeast corner of the courthouse grounds. Mr. Will Hammonds arrived in town early enough to park his car in the same spot on the main street of town and then take his place on the same bench every week. Wearing a broad-brimmed straw hat, he spoke to people as they walked by and frequently engaged walkers in conversations. One of our neighbors said that Mr. Hammonds was "holding court." People said that Mr. Will's absence from his courtyard bench meant that someone had taken "his parking place" and that he'd returned to his home in the heart of Saddletree… upset.

From the courthouse square to the fire station several blocks away, I could hear the sounds of multiple people greeting one another and laughing loudly, listen in on snippets of conversation, see mamas of all colors disciplining their children, hear car engines sputter and roar, and get stopped cold in my tracks by the occasional backfire from a vehicle. It was a far different world from the quiet countryside I knew a mere seven miles away.

By noontime or so, we were usually done with our errands, so we'd head home to Saddletree. But sometimes Daddy would ask, "Lena, how'd you like to ride across the river and see if we can find a hot dog?"

My face always erupted into a grin, and my lips always replied, "Oh yes!"

Our ride toward the river didn't take long, for Lumberton was a small town. Soon, we'd reach West Second Street, pass the *Robesonian* building (the local newspaper), and begin to drive over the bridge spanning the Lumber River. As always, I'd try to look straight ahead to avoid seeing any of the waters of the river. The thoughts of deep water made me nervous, which was the natural outgrowth of a child who couldn't swim and who'd heard stories about bodies being dragged out dead from this very river we were crossing. As always, the stories about the dreaded snakes dropping into boats surfaced, too.

A left turn just beyond the intersection of West Second Street and the Fairmont Highway and we were there. The Stallings Grill was right in front of the bumper of our vehicle. The steam from the grill inside was so thick that it often made the interior of the café look foggy through the large glass windows on the front of the building. The steam-covered windows never completely hid the view of the long counter with bar stools and people cooking and serving the hot food that was causing the windows to look foggy.

I'd wait in whatever vehicle we came in for my dad to go inside, buy our lunch, and bring it out. The Stallings Grill probably served all kinds of sandwiches, but steaming hot dogs were the only food I ever saw purchased there: as many as you could afford or your dad would buy. They were ten cents each.

My dad ate his two hot dogs the way he liked them: with mayonnaise, onions, salt, and pepper. He washed them down with a Nehi orange drink, one name we called sodas or soft drinks, while I ate one hot dog and drank a NuGrape. Folks passing by didn't know it, but if they saw Dad and me, they were seeing two people who were "living high on the hog." That's what I thought, even though I wasn't completely sure what the phrase meant. I believed the phrase was about having enough money to do what one wanted. That surely fit this occasion.

Too soon, the hot dogs and "bottle drinks," our favorite name for commercially prepared nonalcoholic beverages, were consumed. It was time for Daddy and me to begin the return ride to our home in the country. His errands were done, our stomachs were full, and I was happy. And the best part of it all was the ride across the river with my dad.

<hr/>

My parents knew that what children don't see or experience on a regular basis fascinates them. They knew that my going to town was not only fun but also an educational experience and that riding across the river to the Stallings Grill to eat was a special treat for me. My parents prolonged the joys of rides across the river and postponed the pain of revealing the real reasons why Daddy and I rode across the river to Stallings Grill to eat.

Until we got older, my brothers and I were unaware of the café on Fourth Street, the only place in downtown Lumberton where Indians were allowed to buy food. The café was an unattractive "walk-in, walk-out" establishment where customers walked in, ordered and paid for food, and then walked out and ate while standing or walking on the street as the many Saturday town visitors meandered by. The environment was less than ideal for a family dining experience. It was a glaring example of separation and discrimination.

From the time I began to read when I was almost five years old, I saw and read the signs that many restaurants in town openly displayed that read WHITE ONLY. Though I saw them, I didn't ask about them. Mama and Daddy didn't talk about them, either, when I was young. I knew I was *not* a white person, and the message of the signs was clear: Indians are not allowed in these places.

From a distance, the significance of those rides across the river was not about discrimination, nor was it a lesson about racism and exclusion. Instead, those rides across the river were a demonstration of wise and loving parents providing time and space for a child to grow and develop with an inclusive love, constant care, and a young mind wide open to the possibilities that life held.

My parents knew that innocence mixed with confusion often leads to inner turmoil that the very young cannot name or understand. But most of all, they feared that any confusion and turmoil in the minds of their young children could develop into a lifelong pattern of dismay, doubt, anger, and hate that would prevent them from leading a positive, productive life with all kinds of people, including those who were white. My parents hoped that their way would prevent this from happening to my brothers and me.

So Franklin, Cam, and I were allowed to be ourselves: young, innocent American Indian children whose lives were filled with happiness and joy. Our parents surrounded us with love, instruction, a simple lifestyle, a positive outlook on life, and personal examples of living as Christians. This, they hoped, would make us less susceptible to the distress and dejection of racism once we met it; we would then know it for what it was.

My rides across the river produced some good lunches and pretty clothes, a few lies, and many cherished memories. More than anything, they helped to prepare me for the variety of roads and rivers I would cross in the days and years to come.

Mama and Movies

*M*ovies are something I can take or leave. As is often the case, this started when I was young. My parents didn't go to the movies, so I didn't, either…for a long time. When I was around eight or nine years old, I was introduced to movies in Pembroke, a small town of fewer than two thousand people about twenty miles west of my home. Some people called Pembroke the Indian capital. I thought it was because so many Indians lived there close together, or maybe it was because Pembroke State College was located there. PSC, as it was called, was the only state-supported college for Indians in the United States at that time.

My maternal grandparents as well as two uncles, an aunt, and their families all lived in Pembroke, so our family went there quite often. I always looked forward to spending time with my cousin Pat Smith, who was a few months younger than I was. She and her family—Uncle Joe, Aunt Lula Jane, and her little brother Mike—lived with our grandparents at the time. While visiting with Mama's family one Saturday afternoon, Cousin Pat suggested that the two of us could go to a movie while our parents and grandparents visited and our little brothers played in the yard. I knew Pembroke had a movie theater, because we passed it every time we went to visit relatives, but I'd never thought about actually going there. Pat said she'd seen movies there before and that we could probably walk there by ourselves.

Because her suggestion came as a surprise, I tried to act as if this were an everyday occurrence for me. I knew that Mama wouldn't let me walk into town by myself. The most distant walk I'd made was to Horace Hardin's store, across Highway 301 from where we lived, to get a loaf of bread. *But this is town*, I thought. I figured that my cousin's attitude must have reflected one of the differences in being a child who lives in town versus one who lives in the country.

Somehow, Pat convinced our mothers that we were mature enough and that it was safe enough for us to walk to the movie theater and be there by ourselves. Aunt Lula and Mama gave us instructions: "Walk straight to the theater. Don't stop and talk to anyone. Behave once you get inside the theater. And come straight back. No dawdling. Walk straight home."

"Oh yes, we'll do exactly as you say," I heard Pat reply.

The surprise I felt took my voice away momentarily. *We could do this*, I thought, *especially the walking part of the instructions*. And with neither my brothers nor Pat's little brother along, the behaving part would be easy.

I was relieved that Mama hadn't revealed the fact that I'd never been to a movie before. I didn't want to appear less grown up than Pat. But it was difficult to act nonchalant about this venture. I tried to cover up my excitement and ignorance about what to expect. Instead of asking Pat questions, my reaction was to become silent.

"Lena, what's wrong with you? Don't you want to go to the movie?" Pat asked.

"Oh sure," I replied.

"Then why don't you act like it?" she asked. "We don't have to go."

"I want to," I said.

It didn't take long to walk to the theater, which was located on Pembroke's short main street. The small ticket office appeared to enclose the ticket seller, and I imagined it was a jail cell. Pat walked up to the ticket office and paid for her ticket, and I did the same. I followed her as we crossed the small lobby of the theater and entered a large, dimly lit room on the main floor. Unaccustomed to the darkness, my eyes went into a blinking frenzy. Suddenly, I wondered if I were going blind. Pat didn't seem to be bothered by any weird eye condition, so I reassured myself that I'd be fine, too. When Pat sat down, I was relieved that I wouldn't have to try to walk while my eyes blinked like a caution light. I was more than ready to sit down and see a movie.

Soon, the gigantic screen exploded with pictures with writing all over them. The screen was much too big, I thought, and we were much too close to it. The images of people were absurdly large; the music was outrageously loud. But it was the volume of the voices that unnerved me. The movie stars talked far louder than anyone should. I was just overwhelmed.

The story line of the movie didn't make much of an impression on me. Maybe the laughing, talking, and yelling of the people in the theater kept me from following the plot carefully. I was aghast that people who had paid to see the movie were making so much noise. I left the theater more confused than entertained.

"How'd you like the movie, Lena?" my mother asked when we got home.

"Fine, just fine," I replied.

A year or two later, Noyal Ann Hunt, my best friend at the time, called and invited me to go to the movie in Lumberton with her. Her older brother or another family member would provide transportation. All I had to do was get permission from my mother.

"No, Lena, you may not go to the movie this afternoon," my mom said.

"Why not?" I asked.

"Your dad and I don't think going to movies on Sunday is appropriate. Sunday is a day of worship and rest."

No argument I could think of would prevail over what Mama thought would please the Lord. I didn't even try.

It wasn't long before Noyal Ann again invited me to attend a movie with her, and this time it wasn't Sunday. I remembered, too, that Mama had had no other objection to me going. I approached her with a positive mind and a polite mouth. "Mama, would it be OK if I went to the movie with Noyal Ann this afternoon?"

She looked at me with gentle eyes. Then she looked away. Finally, she spoke. "What do you know about the movie theaters in Lumberton?" she asked.

"Nothing much," I said. "They show movies. I know several people who go to see them."

She remained silent for several seconds. Her Adam's apple moved up and down twice as I waited for her to speak. "Lena, your dad and I don't really have anything against movies," she said, "as long as they're appropriate for your age." She paused. "But we don't like some things that go on at the theaters."

My brain went into a frenzy. What could she mean? Surely, there wasn't any drinking at movie theaters. I didn't think so. "I don't know what you mean, Mama," I said.

"Well, I'm going to tell you," she responded. "Whites, blacks, and Indians aren't allowed to sit together. White people go in the main entrance and sit downstairs; Indians and blacks have to enter from a side entrance. Our people and black people have to sit upstairs in the balcony."

Again, she paused and looked at me with her serious catlike eyes. Her eye color seemed to change instantly from gray to green before she continued. "Your dad and I don't like this arrangement. Everyone should sit wherever they wish. Paying the same amount of money and then having to sit upstairs just isn't right. That's why we don't go to the movies in Lumberton."

What Mama said didn't really surprise me. Our daily life was separate in many ways: schools, churches, restaurants, bus stations, and even the water fountains at the courthouse were all marked and separated for use by white, black, and Indian people. It surprised me that Mama seemed pained by voicing the opinion she and Daddy shared about going to the movies in town.

That surprise wasn't the only one our conversation generated, though. Mama looked at me with gray eyes for a moment and spoke. "I understand that you want to be with your friend. I also understand that change comes slowly. Just remember that where you sit in a theater has nothing to do with your worth as a person. You may go to the movie, but remember what I just said."

Well, of course it doesn't, I thought. *I am me, Lena Epps. Going to a movie won't change me or who I am in any way.*

Once Noyal Ann and I were seated in the balcony of the Carolina Theater and engrossed in the movie, it was easy to forget Mama's little talk. It was only once I'd noticed the low partition separating Indian people from black people that I thought about what she'd said. But just for a moment.

On the way out of the theater, I did look over the balcony railing to the main floor to see how it looked. The downstairs space appeared much larger than the balcony, and I could see some pretty light fixtures on the walls. Overall, it looked the same as the upstairs. We all watched the same movie on the one big screen. It took a few moments before I realized the major difference between the downstairs and balcony sections of the theater: there were no partitions on the main floor. But so what? That's just the way it was. Mama had told me about this. I thought nothing more of it.

Going to the movies didn't become a weekly occurrence in my life. I did attend often enough—sometimes with my brothers and less frequently with friends—that both the Carolina and Riverside theaters became familiar Lumberton sites to me. Quite soon, I learned that restrooms weren't available for Indians in the theaters. I guessed that this was true for black people as well. I wondered briefly if anyone upstairs had ever had a restroom accident. That, I decided quickly, wasn't anything to think about for long.

My brothers seemed to enjoy going to the movies more than I did. They especially like the shoot-'em-up variety, which I didn't care for at all. The blood and the killings didn't appeal to me. And there was one other thing: I didn't relate to the Indians in the movies at all. Feathers in their hair? Grunting instead of speaking? Fighting with everyone? The movie Indians seemed to be from another world, another time, or maybe just another state. For sure, the movie Indians were not about me or my people. So I either avoided them or tuned them out.

The best thing about movies was being with a cousin or a friend. But, as Mama always said, "There's nothing like a good book. You can travel, learn new things, meet new people, and imagine a different kind of life." And, she always pointed out, "Books don't require admission fees or needing to have someone take you anywhere."

Some movies were fun, but a good book was usually better entertainment for me. Mama knew me well.

Hot Dogs on the Road

*W*hile hot dogs were probably never the featured entrée at any fine restaurant in North Carolina in the distant days of the '40s and '50s, as a child during that time, I believed that any good restaurant would serve them. The fear of too much fat, sodium, or calories was unknown, at least to me. Hot dogs were just good to eat.

At our home on the grounds of Magnolia School, in rural northern Robeson County, hot dogs were not often part of our daily diet. Rather, they were an occasional supper that provided a delightful change for my brothers and me from our usual meal of meat, vegetables, and bread. Preparing the hot dogs was easy, but according to Mama, the process required two specific steps. First, the weenies (what we called the little round uncooked pieces of meat) had to be boiled. As soon as the water began to gurgle, I stood ready to proceed with what I claimed to be my job.

"They're not ready yet," Mama said. "They have to boil for a while. When they float up near the top of the water and are plump, you can check them. Stand right here and don't let them boil over."

I paid close attention to the boiling weenies. When they were so fat that it looked as if the casings would pop or the weenies might explode, I asked Mama if I could perform the second step of hot-dog preparation. That was giving the weenies the doneness test. A dinner fork would provide the answer. I poked a fork into the weenies and was rewarded with a line of clear juice coming out of them. According to Mama, the weenies were done.

Mama seemed to be the only person concerned about cooking the hot dogs properly. Daddy liked hot dogs, cold or hot, and he was very specific about how he liked to eat them. Plenty of mayonnaise, onions, salt, and pepper on his weenie wrapped in a slice of white bread made the perfect hot dog. None of the condiments were necessary for his three children. Just bring on the hot dogs! If we had hot dog buns, then that would be a special treat. No matter what the weenies were wrapped in, I was certain I could eat more hot dogs than I was given.

The novelty of having hot dogs for supper was reason enough to be pleasantly surprised, but that was nothing compared to the really big treat we were in for once or twice a year. The great event began with an announcement by my dad that we were "going up home" to visit his family in Person County. The excitement and anticipation would build from there. The journey, of more than 150 miles, was the equivalent of a cross-country trip to those of us who were unaccustomed to traveling much more than twenty miles from home. We would travel for at least six hours and see towns, cities, and countryside that were far different from the sandy flatlands we knew. My brothers and I would count cows, horses, cars, and trucks until we were tired or I got mad because of them cheating. I knew they couldn't count that fast. I couldn't, and I'd had more practice than they did.

The best part of a trip to Person County was that our family would have a picnic on the way. On that one day, eating supper would not mean having a meal that included one vegetable that at least one child absolutely detested. Our parents would be spared the drudgery of hearing a passionate monologue aimed to convince the others that they, too, shared a dislike for whatever Mama had prepared. We could, for the most part, forget about table manners as well. If things worked out as we hoped, we'd have hot dogs to eat. Make no mistake about it: that would be the highlight of the trip.

Finally, the big day would come. We usually began our travels in the late afternoon after school on Friday, or on the day after Christmas. My brothers and I sat in the back seat trying ever so hard to be well-behaved, as we'd promised. Our parents probably prayed that our promises to behave would last till picnic time. Neither promises nor prayers were fulfilled. Usually, by the time we got to St. Pauls, only seven miles away, the chant began: "I'm hungry." Franklin, the older of my brothers, always began the pitiful refrain.

"I'm hungry, too." Baby brother Cam joined in soon after "Brother" (the name I often called Franklin) started his lament. It was a duet of dynamic proportions that increased in volume as we rode.

Daddy said one time he believed that the vibrations of the moving car were what induced Brother's hunger. Whatever started it, Mama and Daddy always responded with a look between them that said, "I knew it was coming." We all knew that the chant would end permanently only when the car began its departure off the highway to the spot our dad had chosen for our traveling dining experience.

We had picnics at several places on the way to Person County. Some were just off the main highway, in driveways that led to vacant houses or unused farm buildings. These were quiet places—at least until we got there. Other times we ate at the edge of gas-station parking lots near one of the small towns we drove through on our journey. After Daddy bought gas, he would park our car nearby but out of the way of other customers. Mama passed out the food with a caution to behave, which meant staying close by our car, being fairly quiet, and keeping disagreements to a minimum. That was too much like eating at home!

My favorite picnic spot wasn't very far from home. Daddy would drive into Fayetteville and go halfway around the Market Square, where slaves were sold many years ago. Then he'd head the car north on Highway 401. We traveled past the huge Veterans Hospital, several residential communities, and a few business establishments. Soon we'd be in the country again. In the distance I could see a curve in the road. I knew that my favorite picnic spot was just around that curve, off to the right in a small stand of pine trees. Relatively short, the trees formed a boundary of sorts for the picnic area. Brown pine needles and fallen broom straw made a colorful, crackling carpet for much of the area, though the sandy soil of Cumberland County was underneath. Brushy bushes, a few clumps of grass, and patches of broom straw dotted the area. Broken tree limbs and a few medium-size rocks completed the natural landscape of this special place.

Mama brought out the brown paper bag that contained our surprise supper, and Daddy carried the soft drinks that would replace milk for just that meal. The boys and I explored the picnic site. We checked out the best possible place to sit. Was a grassy spot, a piece of wood, or a stump the best place to eat? We debated where Mama and Daddy would put the food. Often, the only thing we agreed on was the best location for going to the "restroom." Even that could be a point of contention. A big sister needed more privacy than her younger brothers.

Franklin, Cam, and I could only guess what we might eat for our early supper. It might be Mama's pimento cheese sandwiches with homemade filling so thick it looked like orange potato salad. The main attraction could be "boloney" (the way we said and spelled it) sandwiches. Mama made them fat, with thick slices of meat and soft, white Merita bread purchased that day from Horace Hardin's store across Highway 301 from where we lived. We might have a plate of deviled eggs; I always hoped the boys didn't want any. Or would we have a bag of cookies from Swain's grocery in Lumberton? That would definitely be a treat, since store-bought bakery goods were a rare delicacy at our home.

"Oh please, Mama, aren't you just about ready for us to eat? We're about to *starve* to death!"

The voices of Brother, Cam, and me spoke alone and together. They stopped only when we heard Daddy say quietly: "You children pipe down."

That sentence silenced the sounds of our pleas for at least a minute or two.

At last, we were called to eat. Wonder of wonders! Today our fantasy became our reality. It was *hot dogs* for supper. Plain, cold, uncooked weenies wrapped up in a slice of that wonderfully fresh white Merita bread made the best picnic supper one could ever hope to eat. Mayonnaise—unrefrigerated, of course—or mustard was an afterthought and completely unnecessary. Just pass my hot dog, thank you very much!

Whatever else the brown bag contained was secondary. Deviled eggs, OK. Cookies would be fine. We would eat whatever else we were offered, but nothing compared to the sight and taste of those plain, uncooked hot dogs—one package of eight for the five of us. Sorry, Old Foundry Restaurant and Stallings Grill, not even your best could be a close rival.

With our stomachs full, hearts happy, and bladders empty (or so our parents hoped), we would begin the second phase of our trip from Mama's homeland in Robeson to Daddy's heartland in Person. My brothers and I promised, once again, to ride without too much rude or rowdy behavior. All was right in our world, at least for that short time. We'd had hot dogs on the road.

⌒

It never occurred to my brothers and me that our beloved picnics with cold hot dogs resulted from anything other than our parents' desire to provide us with supper and a little adventure on a long car ride. We had no idea that few, if any, cafés or restaurants of any type would serve our American Indian family. It never occurred to us that my dad, with his olive skin, might be considered a black man or that my mother, with her fair skin, might be identified as a white woman. We never knew that the range of our skin colors, from sandy white to dark pecan tones, could be the cause for insults, gunshots, or worse. We didn't know that

Indian and black people were the targets of evil based on something that we accepted was as natural as the morning sun: the colors of our skin.

We were ourselves, the Frank and Grace Epps family, on our way to see relatives who loved us and whom we loved and enjoyed. My brothers and I were young and innocent. We retained our loud laughter, childish antics, and total enjoyment of picnics in pine thickets, gas-station parking lots, and other unusual places. Our parents believed that innocence was better for us at that time in our lives than apprehension, rejection, and fear. Those hot dogs on the road proved they were right.

Innocence-Photographs

Daddy and baby Lena at Mama's college graduation in 1942

Daddy, Mama and fat baby Lena at home in 1943

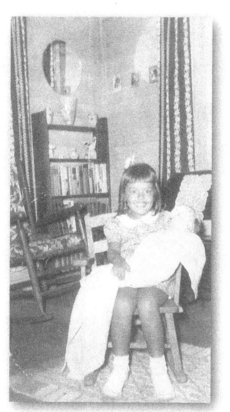

Lena at age five in the living room with her big baby doll

Lena, age seven; Franklin, age three; Cam, age sixteen months had a formal portrait made in St. Pauls. Lena is unhappy with the curls and photographer.

Awareness

Sicker Than Before

No one I ever knew wanted to be sick. I especially dreaded getting sick when I was a little girl. In addition to feeling bad, I was certain that being sick meant resting, and resting wasn't one of my favorite things to do. Resting meant being bored, I believed.

Television hadn't been invented yet, or at least hadn't made its appearance at our home in Saddletree. We had no cartoons or videos to keep a little mind from thinking about not feeling well. We did have a radio in the house, but my parents used that for adult purposes: news, religious programs, and political updates. We didn't have board games, and I wasn't about to try to interest my baby brothers in playing house. Most definitely I would not invite them to play "doll baby" with me, for they had a little destructive streak that I knew might cause some serious damage to my treasured doll babies.

In spite of my generally healthy childhood and dislike of resting, I did get sick occasionally. Most often I suffered from what some in the family called "bad tonsils" and that the doctor diagnosed as tonsillitis. When this or any other unwanted illness occurred, I knew exactly what to expect.

At our home, sick children were treated with compassion, loving care, and specific remedies. Sore throats got a very hot salt-water gargle as the first treatment, and this I tolerated well. Castor oil was terrible and supposedly could do something positive for digestive ailments or elimination problems, though it made me feel nauseated just to think about it. But the worst of all home medications was cod-liver oil. I knew that it would make me much sicker than whatever illness I had or might contract in the future. I thought that swallowing cod-liver oil was a form of death itself and would suffer silently to prevent even hearing mention of that dreaded concoction.

My favorite at-home medicinal aid was one that Mama made herself. Homemade lemonade heated very hot and served in one-cup servings at bedtime was the best medicine I ever took. Some thought it was the lemon juice that made it so effective, and I'm sure that helped. Its real power, however, was in its main ingredient. Hot lemonade was pure, unrefined love. It was so good, one could almost hope not to feel well or to exaggerate the truth about how one felt.

On one of the rare occasions when even hot lemonade didn't cure me or at least make me feel better, my dad took me to a doctor in Lumberton for professional medical attention.

It was a school day, and I was no more than eight years old. Daddy and I climbed a long flight of narrow stairs to reach the doctor's office in a building located across the street from the Robeson County Courthouse on Elm Street, the main street in Lumberton. I seated myself in a straight-back chair while my dad checked in with the staff at the desk. The room was a medium-size one and was full of people. *This doctor must be really busy*, I thought; *look at all these people waiting to see him.* Quickly, my thoughts returned to why I was there. Oh, I hope he doesn't give me a shot or anything like castor or cod-liver oil. Maybe he'll run out of anything bad by the time he sees me.

As I watched the people, my dad talked to the office staff. When he returned to where I was sitting, he said we'd have a wait before the doctor would see us. He then asked if I thought I'd be comfortable sitting alone while he walked a couple of blocks to the bank to attend to some business. He said that his bank business wouldn't take long and that he would return long before it was time for us to be seen by the doctor. He assured me that I didn't need to be afraid of being alone. With that, I agreed to stay. Daddy restated his promise to return quickly, reminded me to behave, and then left for the bank.

I knew how to behave. I would sit quietly and look around at all the other people there. I would read a magazine or book, if one were in my reach. Maybe I'd be lucky and get a child's Bible that had pictures of Jesus and the disciples in it. I would like that. But I knew I wouldn't get up and walk around. That wasn't part of behaving well when you were away from home, according to my parents.

For a short time, I looked at the people in the waiting room. I became aware that all the people had pale skin, and I was the darkest person in the room. But so what? That's just the way it happened to be on this day in this doctor's office. Abruptly, a door opened, and a nurse dressed in all white came out and began to call people's names. She scanned the room, and her eyes seemed to rest on me. I began to get a bit nervous. I didn't want to go back to see the doctor without my dad; I didn't know what to say to a doctor. *Please don't call my name*, I thought, and she didn't.

The nurse continued to look in my direction, and I believed she was staring at me. I began to get uncomfortable. Then I became fearful. Something in this woman's eyes made me want to leave…to run…to hide. But I could do none of those things: I'd promised Daddy I'd wait for him to return.

Quickly, the nurse walked to where I was sitting, stopped in front of me, and demanded in a loud voice, "What are you doing in here?"

I was too scared to reply. I thought that everyone knew why we were all there: we were sick.

"What are you doing in here?" she asked in an even louder, mad-sounding voice.

By now, it seemed that everyone in the room had turned their eyes to me. "My dad brought me to see the doctor," a tiny, soft voice replied.

Was that me talking? And, without warning, tears began to fall from my eyes. They matched the size of my voice: tiny, tiny, with barely any weight to them at all.

"Well, *you* are in the wrong room. *You* don't belong in here. *You* must leave this room now. *You* are in the wrong room."

The nurse stopped speaking and continued to stare at me for what seemed to be an hour. Finally, she turned and walked away from me.

Oh God, I was scared. I was humiliated, I was afraid! I thought I would die on the spot; I felt nauseated. I was terrified and I was embarrassed. But more than anything, I was confused.

The woman at the desk must have heard some or all of the conversation between the nurse in all white and me. Quickly, she called the nurse over to the office portion of the room and told her that I was in the right place, but the nurse disagreed. I listened in shock and horror as the two women discussed where I should sit. I heard words about my being "too dark" to be in this waiting room. As those two voices discussed my skin color and the appropriate place for me to be, I sat silently, immobilized by a pain I'd never felt before. I didn't know the name of the pain, but I felt sick all over. And the tears continued to trickle down my young brown face.

Finally, the nurse in all white left the room. I sat there alone with anguish so large that it seemed that I might be swallowed up whole by it. In fact, that would have been a welcome relief just then. At some point, my tears stopped, my heart started beating more slowly, and my brain went blank. I waited without fear, without hope, and without any expectation of what would happen next. The shock, pain, and confusion of this experience numbed me. I waited for Daddy while in a state of emotional paralysis.

Daddy did come back, but it felt like he was gone forever. After one look at my face, he asked me what was wrong. All I could manage to say was that the nurse had said I didn't belong in this room. The uninvited tears began to trickle again. There were no sobs, just tears on my young brown face.

The look on Daddy's face was a picture of things I'd never seen before. I guessed that he was angry with the nurse for the unkind words she'd spoken to me. I didn't realize until I was older that what I'd seen on his face was also unspoken grief for the pain his young daughter had suffered and for which he had no real cure.

Quietly, very quietly, he talked and I listened. He told me that the nurse was wrong, wrong, wrong. He said that she'd made a bad mistake and that I did belong in that waiting room. He would make certain, he said, that everyone there knew that the nurse had made a mistake. I listened without responding and watched as he walked to the office area of the room.

He didn't yell or even talk in a loud voice. He was, as always, dignified and courteous. As he discussed the situation with the woman in the office area, it was clear to all in the room, including me, that Daddy considered what had happened an act of serious misbehavior. It was, he said, especially wrong that anyone would direct such inappropriate comments toward a child. His shock and outrage were visible, and the woman was very apologetic.

When Daddy came back to where I was sitting, his demeanor was quieter still. Perhaps it was my imagination, but he seemed to be sad. Never a man to lie or exaggerate, he said only that the office woman knew that a terrible mistake had been made and that she was sorry. With a gentle voice, he concluded by saying, "As I told you earlier, this room is exactly where you're supposed to be. Do you understand?"

Of course, I heard what my dad said, and I understood the meaning of his words of reassurance. Whether I believed them completely, I wasn't sure. What mattered most was that Daddy was there. He had defended me in the presence of danger and pain. He had kept me from further harm.

Together, we waited in silence for our turn to see the doctor. What the doctor said to either my dad or me is lost forever. I don't know what diagnosis he made or what medicine, if any, he prescribed. Whatever was wrong with me when I went there didn't compare with the dull heartache that lingered long after I left. I didn't know at the time that I had experienced, in full force, the side effects of one of the deadliest diseases known to humankind: racism.

Even Mama's hot lemonade, loaded with love and sugar, wasn't strong enough to relieve the pain I felt after I left the doctor's office and returned home. Yes, I was sicker than before Daddy had taken me to town to be made well.

Durham Dogs

When I was around ten years old, our family was again on the road to visit our Epps grandparents in northern Person County. The High Plains community, to be exact. Mama and Daddy told us before we left home that we wouldn't have a picnic on the way. We would eat in Durham, and we could have hot dogs there. It really wasn't what we'd hoped to hear, because nothing could compare to a picnic with our special hot dogs.

No doubt we complained. We claimed, as we often did while riding in a car for more than fifteen minutes, that our stomachs growled for food. From a brown paper bag, Mama offered apples, an orange to share, and some crackers. "This will tide you over till we get to Durham," she said.

"Just hold on for a while," Daddy said.

It was dark when we reached Durham. The lights of North Carolina Central College brightened Highway 55 as we passed by. When we passed the Epes Trucking Company (we always pointed out that the Epps name was misspelled), Daddy told us what we wanted to hear. It wouldn't be long before we'd get to the restaurant where he planned to stop for us to eat. Soon afterward, we came to the Braggtown neighborhood, which appeared to be a pleasant part of Durham. It wasn't fancy, but the small to medium-size houses looked well maintained. Several churches, a school, and a variety of small businesses were located on or near Roxboro Road, also named Highway 55, the road on which we traveled through part of Durham en route to Person County.

"We're almost to the café where we'll eat. You can fill your bellies with hot dogs or whatever you like," Daddy said.

Well, that was just fine with us! My little brothers and I could barely contain our excitement.

As Daddy slowed the car and began to turn off Roxboro Road, we recognized this place. It was an older, whitish-gray, and rectangular-shaped building that housed both a tiny grocery store of sorts and a café. Close to the street, bins of fruits, vegetables, and nuts outside the structure marked the grocery store side. The café side was farther from the street and had ample space for cars to park and use the drive-in service for food.

While Dad parked the car, I remembered other times when we'd stopped here. On those visits, Daddy and Mama went into the little grocery store, and my brothers and I stayed in the car. Daddy always purchased fresh fruit and a loaf of bread; many times, he also bought meat and nuts to take to his parents. If it were winter, he usually bought fresh vegetables as well. After all, there'd be five extra people to feed, and Daddy never wanted our visits to impose any additional hardship on Grandmother and Granddaddy Epps. The fresh fruit was a special treat for Grandmother because she was diabetic, and Granddaddy always received a box of Black Moriah chewing tobacco plugs. If we were lucky, they'd buy us a small surprise: a bar of candy, a pack of chewing gum, or something else that we didn't often have at home.

Daddy and Mama left us in the car while they shopped. The boys and I talked about what we were going to order for supper from the drive-in café. There were so many choices: hot dogs, hamburgers, milkshakes. We waited patiently for our parents to return to the car with their purchases, but we quickly became impatient after Daddy drove the car to the café side of the establishment. We'd never been to the drive-in café before.

We waited for one of the curb boys to come and take our order. No one approached our car. We waited longer still. Squirming and hanging over the back of the front seat, we watched as the curb boys stood at the front of the building doing nothing. But finally, here comes one headed our way. The boy walked a bit closer to our car and looked directly at us. Then, he turned around and walked back to the café. He stood with the small group of his fellow curb boys at the front of the drive-in. They talked to one another and glanced our way several times.

"What's taking him so long to come out here, Daddy?" one of the little brothers asked.

"He must've forgotten his order pad," Dad replied.

"Can I have a milkshake?" asked the other little brother.

After what seemed to be a very long time, the young man, who appeared to be about sixteen or seventeen, came to the driver's door. Daddy rolled down the window and immediately placed our order. For a split second there was silence. The curb boy wrote nothing on his pad before he spoke.

"We don't serve niggers."

The young white curb boy had hurled a lethal bomb of racial evil at the Frank Epps family. It exploded without a sound and filled the car with its ugliness. Our family felt its impact as one. We were stunned by the words of discrimination that were filling our ears. We were shocked by the fumes of hate, injustice, and ignorance permeating our bodies. We were injured by this attack, but the injuries didn't show; the damage was internal. A few seconds later, the pain began to hurt. My heart constricted with outrage, anger, and fear. Stunned and unable to do anything else, my brothers and I began to cry.

"What do you mean?" my dad demanded angrily. "Look at this arm." He stuck his arm outside the open window and rolled his shirt sleeve up several inches. "This is the arm of an American Indian. It is brown. Look at it. It is brown. It is not black; it is not colored. Do you understand that? It's been a long time since anyone made this kind of mistake about me."

Barely stopping to take a breath, Daddy continued: "I stopped here to get food for my wife and children. They're hungry. I didn't stop to be insulted or to have my family insulted. I don't aim to repeat all that I just said." Daddy then spoke louder and with more anger in his voice than I'd ever heard. "This is what we will have," Dad said.

He then told the mean white boy what we wanted to eat…again. The crying from the back seat intensified.

The white curb boy stood as silent and rigid as a mummy for a short while. He mumbled something about making a mistake. Then he turned and walked back to the café. When he reached the other curb boys, they talked for a few minutes, turning to look our way a couple of times. Finally, the curb boy who'd been at our car went inside.

Mama sat with her shoulders straight and said nothing. She seemed to be staring at something far past the front door of the drive-in café. Daddy rolled up the window, rolled down his sleeve, and said nothing more. The crying of the children continued. Our parents seemed frozen, unable to speak or move. The five of us were bonded together by birth blood and racial torment.

Perhaps our parents asked us to stop crying. Maybe they offered words of comfort or explanation. I don't remember. My brothers and I did quit crying, finally. The silence in the car was unnatural and uneasy. Even the air was weird. It was heavy, almost too heavy to breathe. I was ready to leave Durham and never, ever return. How much time passed is a mystery to me.

Finally my dad spoke: "Here comes our food."

"Well, then, it's time to eat," Mama said.

The lunch-size bags of food passed from the white hands of the curb boy to the brown hands of my father. Daddy passed the bag with the chicken-salad sandwich to my mother's pale-skinned hand. She took her long-awaited coffee with cream in her other pale hand. Turning to the back seat, Daddy held a bag and said, "Here are your hot dogs. You can fill up those stomachs now."

"We're not hungry," three young voices replied in unison.

"Of course you're hungry," said Mama.

"We're not hungry."

"Well, it's way past suppertime, and it's still a long ride to Person County. You'd better eat while you can." Dad's voice was firm and soft. Still, my brothers and I refused the food.

Mama added, "You need to forget what that boy said. Just don't pay attention to him at all. *He was acting ignorant.* Now, just go ahead and eat."

"We're not hungry." Again, the three of us spoke together.

Durham hot dogs were not appealing to us. They were seasoned with meanness and color poison. Any hot dog that caused our dad to get angry and caused us to cry just wasn't fit to eat. So we didn't eat hot dogs or anything else. By now, our parents likely realized that hunger was no longer of concern in the back seat. Hunger had been replaced with pain in their children. Brother, Cam, and I were all hurting from an illness whose name we didn't know. But our parents knew its name was racism and that two of its common side effects were lack of appetite and loss of laughter.

Mama and Daddy sat up front and ate their food, silently. Franklin, Cam, and I sat in the heavy air of the back seat. For once, not one of us had anything to say. But I had plenty to think about. Was I the reason this white boy had said bad things to my dad? I knew that I had the darkest skin of anyone in my family. That mean, impolite boy made it sound like we were all unwelcome there. Still, I wondered if he really meant just me. The question replayed in my head like a stuck 78-rpm record.

"It's time to head up the road," Dad announced.

There was no last-minute reminder about going to the bathroom or making sure we'd wiped our faces and hands properly. No one said a word about the food we'd eaten or left untouched. The only sounds I heard were of my own heart beating wildly and in my head the repetition of "Did I cause this"?

Soon, we were away from Durham and out in the country on Highway 501 north, riding toward the red clay soil of the High Plains community. The nasty remains of racism lingered in the car long after we left Durham, as did the question in my head. Worn out by it all, I curled into a corner of the back seat and tried to sleep. The words of the stuck 78-rpm record continued to play. Had my brown skin caused this terrible experience?

No answer came for that question. And as hard as I tried, I could not remove it from my mind. But one thing was certain: there were mean people—those who judged people by their skin color—in Durham, far away from Robeson County. I realized then that there were probably people everywhere who would look at me and decide I was black. Those people would try to make my life miserable. There would be no eating out at restaurants, no going to movies, no doing anything away from home if white people were involved. All because of my brown skin. I wasn't sure which hurt more: my stomach or my heart.

My little brothers quickly went to sleep, and it was quiet in the front seat, too. I was silent but awake. How mean and foolish could people be? And just how long would I feel sick all over because of Durham and hot dogs? I drifted off to sleep sometime before I knew the answer.

For many people, hot dogs are nothing more than a poor kind of sustenance for the physical body. Loaded with calories, fat, and sodium, they convert into quick energy that we use for whatever activity comes next, and then it's time for something more substantial. Hot dogs in my childhood did more than create energy. One kind of hot dog, those enjoyed on picnics with my family, provided love, acceptance, safety, and sweet memories. Plain, cold hot dogs kept our young hearts and minds innocent and happy, untouched by the pain of prejudice and the power of discrimination that Jim Crow laws produced and prolonged. Our parents knew something others hadn't learned: *cold hot dogs were health foods for the bodies and souls of Indian children on the road.*

The Durham hot dogs introduced the pain of prejudice to my brothers and reemphasized it to me. We discovered that ignorance and injustice often lurk in unexpected places and that one cannot be totally prepared for their sudden appearance. My brothers learned that a taste of ignorance or injustice will sicken a young child's heart more than it hurts a stomach.

Without realizing it, my brothers and I witnessed a nightmare for loving, caring parents like ours: They heard the blood of their blood and the love of their lives cut down with words of derision and insult. They listened as the blood of their ancestors was misidentified and mocked with words of hostility and loathing. They endured the desecration of their people by a youngster filled with contempt and disrespect.

We were unaware of it at the time, but Franklin, Cam, and I learned life lessons in Durham that became embedded in our minds and hearts forever. We saw and heard how our parents handled a racial crisis: Our parents didn't run from a bad situation. Both kept their emotions in control. One person spoke for the group. My father stated how he felt and what he expected to happen. He made no derogatory comments about the race of the person who had caused us distress. He provided a brief explanation that was appropriate for those involved. The situation was silent history when it was over.

Perhaps the most important lesson we learned in Durham was this: A race-poisoned hot dog didn't kill my brothers or me. Our parents wouldn't allow us to digest the "whole dog" without a powerful antidote. Their antidote to racial poison was the acknowledgment that race hating was ignorant and wrong and the provision of a great amount of love and support. Life would go on in spite of prejudice, pain, and people who made life difficult.

Years went by, and I no longer actively thought about Durham and hot dogs. But buried deep within my being, the tiny seeds of distrust and fear lived still. Time and tender care from those who loved me healed the pain of poison hot dogs. In fact, the bad hot dog episode in Durham helped to create an emotional supplement that caused my brothers and me to grow stronger. As is the case with many serious injuries, however, the scars of those wounds remained forever.

Hot dogs in the woods or hot dogs in Durham? For me, there was nothing like time spent in God's great outdoors, especially with a weenie wrapped in soft Merita bread and surrounded by love and laughter. Pass my plain, uncooked hot dog, please.

Movies Matter

In the summer of 1954, just after I'd finished the seventh grade, Daddy invited my brothers and me to accompany him to Whiteville, the county seat and largest town in Columbus County, about thirty-five miles from home. Daddy's suggestion that the three of us could go to a movie while he tended to business was a surprise. We were ready to go long before he was ready to leave.

"Walk up to the ticket booth and buy your tickets," Daddy said. "Then, walk into the lobby and buy one large box of popcorn and a drink. After you get your refreshments, go into the big movie auditorium, find yourselves seats, and enjoy the movie. You boys, mind your 'little mama.' I'll be sitting in the car when you come out of the theater."

We did just as Daddy instructed. It was cool and comfortable inside the lobby. The light from the wall sconces and the movie screen, the only sources of light, made the auditorium-like room on the main floor quite dark. I led the way, and we quickly found seats. I sat near the aisle with baby brother Cam next to me, and Brother Franklin sat on Cam's left side. I began the task of passing our refreshments to the boys and hoped that they would share quietly and without spilling the drink or popcorn.

The featured movie was beginning when I felt a touch on my left shoulder. I looked around and heard the voice of a man standing nearby.

"Y'all are going to have to go upstairs," the stranger said.

By this time I could see that the man was white and tall and had slick black hair.

"What?" I asked with a sinking heart.

"You have to go upstairs with the colored people. Now!"

"What's he saying?" Cam asked.

"We've got to move. Come on. Now," I said.

"What are you talking about?" Brother asked Cam.

"Tell Brother to get up, and y'all come on. Now! I'll tell you why later," I whispered. "Just come on *now.*"

This total stranger, the tall white man with slicked-back black hair, led us back to the lobby. He pointed to the stairs at the side of the room. "Go on up there; that's where you belong." His voice was clear and cold, like ice.

My hands shook, and my heart beat wildly. A big, hard lump was lodged in my throat. I couldn't see clearly, and my knees felt weak. I wanted to cry, but that lump in my throat kept any sound from coming out. Anyway, that would only humiliate me further.

What if I passed out? I thought. *I can't pass out. Yes, I can. I could just die right now. No, you can't. Yes, I can. Somebody's got to take care of Brother and Cam. Oh Lordy, that's me. How much further till we can sit down? I don't want to sit down. Well, you have to.* "You boys be quiet. We're almost there." I said those words without knowing what my brothers said. I was focused on taking one step at a time without stumbling or doing something worse.

The balcony of the theater had no partitions. We sat down as the tall white man with slicked-back black hair watched from the top of the stairs. He didn't come into the balcony seating area. The few black people who were there turned their attention from the movie to us.

"What you doing up here?" a young man asked. I said nothing. "You in the wrong place," he added.

"Leave 'em alone," another voice said.

Yes, please leave us alone, I thought. *I want everyone to leave us alone, including that tall white man with the slicked-back black hair. I want somebody to come here right now and hurt him. I want somebody to come here and force him to apologize for making me feel ashamed and afraid. I want to somehow just be out of here.*

Again, Cam asked about why we'd had to move. Brother Franklin asked for more popcorn.

"Just share the popcorn and drink. We'll talk about why we had to change seats after the movie's over," I whispered.

They accepted that without further questions and settled in to watch the movie.

I wanted to cry. I wanted to be far away from all of this big mess. But I was trapped with my little brothers. We couldn't leave; we had nowhere to go. We had to wait for Daddy, and that wouldn't be for a while. I sat in the silent hell that the movie theater had quickly become. The movie was a loud blur; my mind was a silent blank.

"Did you children have a good time at the movie?" We had barely gotten into the car when Daddy asked the dreaded question. Cam and Franklin told their version of what had happened. Just hearing them talk about it made me feel small and insecure. The lump in my throat was getting larger again. *Oh please!* I thought. *Don't let me throw up or cry now.*

"Is this true, Lena?" Daddy asked.

"Yes," I whispered.

My eyes looked far beyond the interior of the car as silence engulfed us all. Daddy looked toward the theater and then back at me. His small brown hands encircled the steering wheel tightly.

"I thought it would be all right for you and the boys to go to the movie here. It should be right anywhere, anytime," he said.

"I'm sorry this happened." There was a pause. "I'm sorry."

Oh Daddy, I thought. *I'm sorry, too. It's not your fault. I don't know whose fault it is, but I know it's not yours.* My thoughts raced on. *I hate being singled out because of my brown skin. I think Franklin and Cam would have been OK if I hadn't been there. I hate this sinking, trembling feeling that I have inside me right now. I wish I could do something to pay back that man for what he did to me...to us.* Then I thought, *I hate every single bit of all of this.*

Before we got to the Robeson County line, I decided that movies didn't matter that much after all. I didn't have to go to any. Nobody would make me go. Nothing mattered now except getting home.

⟶

*O*f course, I did go to the movies again. I went to the Carolina and the Riverside theaters in Lumberton. My girlfriends and I, and sometimes my brothers and I, climbed the stairs to the Indian section of the balconies of both theaters. Sporadically, my cousins and my brothers and I went to the Pembroke Theater, where we sat wherever we chose. We enjoyed whatever appeared on the big screen (or we told our parents we did). We entered the world of fantasy in Robeson County without fear. We knew and followed the rules that our little world required.

One summer day in 1955, Mama totally surprised me by suggesting that the two of us go to Fayetteville to do some shopping. "After we finish shopping," she said, "I thought we might go to a movie."

Shocked, I stood and stared at her. The entire Whiteville episode appeared out of nowhere. All of a sudden, I didn't feel well. I hoped Mama wouldn't notice.

"You're thinking about Whiteville, aren't you? I know that was a terrible experience for you. Your dad was very upset about it. So was I."

I said nothing. She squared her shoulders, and I knew she had more to say.

"There will always be ignorant people in the world, Lena. There will always be mean people. Some of them will try to hurt you because you're an Indian. Mostly, they'll do it with words. The important thing is to make sure you remember that they are either ignorant or mean. It has nothing to do with the kind of person you are or your worth as a person. *Don't ever forget this.*"

She paused. I knew she was right. I also knew she hadn't finished yet.

"You will find that there are places where people will accept you just the way you are. Remember Boone? That's how it should be. That's the way it will be everywhere, someday. Your dad and I hope and pray it will be soon. Now, let's get ready to go to Fayetteville. I'll be with you. I don't expect anything will happen there, but if it does, I'll be with you. We'll do this together."

There was no choice to be made. Not really. Mama knew I was afraid, but she also knew I wanted to be brave. I didn't want to be hurt again. Nor did I wish to be a coward. I would show that man in Whiteville. He could boss me around in Columbus County, but we weren't going there. I just hoped nobody like him worked at the movie theater in Fayetteville.

My nerves were on edge as Mama and I stood at the ticket booth of the movie theater on Hay Street in Fayetteville. I don't think I walked to where we seated ourselves on the main floor of the theater. Maybe I just floated in. Mama smiled at me often. I tried to feel as comfortable as she appeared while the movie flashed on the screen, but it was impossible to relax completely with my heart half frozen with anxiety. When the movie finally ended, I had no desire to watch the previews for the coming attractions.

Mama and I walked to the car lost in our private thoughts. *Nothing happened*, I thought; *nothing happened. Thank goodness, nothing happened.* The singsong of that phrase repeated itself over and over in my head. Slowly, I realized that my heart didn't feel too tight. I felt more natural than I had in hours.

We reached Highway 301 south before Mama spoke. "Now, that wasn't so bad, was it? I told you there were places where we'd have absolutely no problems at all."

I nodded my head in agreement. No problems at all, Mama; no problems at all.

There would be movies I saw later that I remembered, and there would be movies I forgot. None mattered more than the ones I saw before I entered high school. Some of them mattered entirely too much.

The Look of Beauty

Beauty was a way of life for my mother. She saw beauty in a variety of things and places and pointed it out with childlike wonder. Blooming japonicas hanging heavily on the bushes in her mother's front yard caused her to stop and admire them. She appreciated the stained-glass windows in the First Methodist Church in Pembroke, where mostly Indian people, including her mother and other family members, worshipped. Genuine awe filled her voice when she described the paintings she'd seen in the National Gallery of Art in Washington, DC.

In addition to things, certain places entranced her with their beauty. The waves rolling in on the shore of any North Carolina beach caused her to smile and marvel like a little girl. The grand majesty of the mountains in western North Carolina never ceased to amaze her, and the mystery of the "Brown Mountain Lights" added to the wonder of these old creations made by the God she loved.

My dad's view of beauty focused on God's natural creation. He cherished the red clay dirt in High Plains, his birth community, and the taste of the clear spring water he drank as a child. He loved the sight and smell of Person County cedar trees long after he left the county. Rich soil that produced crops was a thing of beauty to him, as were the tall trees of the Robeson County woods he loved to roam. He marveled at the stars, the moon, and the wonder of seeing snow fall to the ground. Even the murky waters of both Big and Raft Swamps, where he hunted with his coon dogs, held a certain fascination for him.

He rarely spoke about his delight in beauty, but one never doubted that he saw beauty and that it affected him. Most often it was a certain look in his eyes: a tiny sparkle or a gaze of awe that acknowledged that he was in the midst of beauty created by a power that exceeded human understanding or replication. Anything prefaced with "Just look at that," was reason enough to stop and visually soak in whatever he pointed out, for he didn't waste words or make conversation just to be talking.

Such were my understandings of beauty when I was a child. People's appearance was absent from the list of things my parents talked about in terms of beauty. At least I never heard them remark on a person's appearance as being beautiful, handsome, or ugly. Nor did I hear them talk about people's racial characteristics in either approving or disapproving terms. In fact, my mother made it perfectly clear that, from her perspective, a person's external appearance was totally unimportant. For her view on physical appearance was quite simple: *pretty is as pretty does.* If I heard it once, I heard it a hundred times before I finished high school. My dad, ever the silent one, often nodded his head in agreement.

That did not mean that Mama didn't pay attention to cleanliness and acceptable attire. When she complimented me on my shining hair or said that I looked nice in my Sunday clothes, I was pleased. I interpreted this as meaning that I'd passed her strict standards for body cleanliness or proper attire. As far as I was concerned, that was the ultimate standard about my appearance when I was a very young girl. What more could matter than Mama's approval?

My parents' lack of interest in or focus on physical beauty didn't prevent me from developing ideas about it. After all, I was a growing girl, and beauty and ugliness and whatever was in between were very much part of that scene. Like all children who read magazines or the newspaper or spent time dreaming of Santa bringing clothes or toys from the department store catalogues of Sears and Penney's, I became aware of the people who were models. I was aware of the many billboards that dotted the fields and banks of Highway 301 as well. All the models were white and attractive.

When I was eight or nine years old, I decided that my mother, in addition to those paid models of beauty, was also pretty. Standing about five foot five with very thick brown hair, green/blue/hazel eyes, skin the color of the sand at Wrightsville Beach, and a very slim figure, she could have been a model in one of those Sears catalogs that I knew from memory. When I told her this, she listened quietly and replied, "Well, I don't know about that. Just remember: it's what's inside that counts." Of course, I knew she was referring to the beauty of the spirit that was based on church teachings, which were sacred in our home. I wouldn't argue with her on that. But I persisted in expressing my opinion about her physical appearance, since I wanted her to acknowledge that she was pretty. Much to my dismay, her response had nothing to do with what I considered beauty. "As long as I'm clean and presentable," she said, "I'm fine with how I look. Just remember"—and I knew the end of the sentence before she spoke—"it's what's inside that counts."

Well, maybe what's inside mattered to all mothers, and that was fine, but I was aware of outward appearances as well. My best friend in elementary school was pretty. Later, it was a classmate in seventh grade who had boys lined up six deep to walk her to the bus. She was both pretty and had a movie-star body. I wasn't blind. Both girls had dark hair, big brown eyes, and fair skin—a striking combination. I didn't wish to be them, but I did notice their appearances.

When I was around eleven years old, a family friend who lived nearby came to visit. It was a typical Robeson County late-spring day: hot with a brilliant sun. While my mother attended to the needs of my brothers, our neighbor talked to me. In the middle of a conversation about nothing of importance, she stopped and looked at me with great seriousness. "Evelena," she said, "you need to stay out of the sun. You're getting too dark. If you get any darker, people are going to think you're colored."

Stunned into silence, I listened as she continued to talk. She emphasized that if I were going to be outside in the sun, I needed to cover up my arms and legs and wear a hat. She also said she'd told her son the same thing. "Both of you just have to watch it. You'll be too dark before you know it."

Because my mother returned at this point, the conversation between the adults resumed. I sat and thought about our neighbor's words.

Too dark? Well, I knew that my skin got quite a bit darker in the spring and summer. I spent much of my playtime and chore time outdoors, so getting darker in hotter weather seemed natural to me. It hadn't been of concern to my parents, for they had never once mentioned it to me. So why would I think about that?

With lightning speed, my mood changed from astonishment to resentment, and my thoughts reflected that: *If you think your son is getting too dark, then go ahead and make him wear a big hat and a shirt with long sleeves when he's out working in the fields. He'll hate it. He could die from the heat being all wrapped up like that. Then you'll be sorry. What you, Miss Nosy Neighbor, need to do is take care of your own business and let Mama take care of me.*

My astonishment and resentment decreased gradually, but I did think more about this unexpected conversation. I bet Mama would never make me dress like our neighbor suggested. If she or Daddy thought I was getting too dark, they'd tell me. Actually, they would have told me long before. *Anyway*, I thought, *this entire focus on skin color and degrees of darkness is just weird.* I decided to just forget what our busybody neighbor had said.

But I didn't just forget about it. I couldn't. I remembered how the white curb boy in Durham had mistaken Daddy, Mama, and my brothers and me for colored people. That was about dark skin. Even back when that mean nurse had told me to leave the doctor's waiting room, it was all about dark skin. And I do have dark skin.

After a short time of thinking about those experiences, I decided I couldn't think about them or my dark skin any longer. Doing so made me feel unsettled and insecure. For now, I decided, I would place my neighbor's preoccupation with my skin color in a spot of my mind that wasn't quite buried but wasn't clearly visible. It would stay there like a caution sign. At this point, all I wanted to do was go straight ahead without thinking about skin color.

When I was in the seventh grade, I rode to my Smith grandparents' house after school with one of the many teachers at Magnolia who lived in Pembroke. Grandmother and I had talked about my school day and the fact that my mom would pick me up later in the afternoon after attending a work-related meeting. She instructed me to do my homework while she visited with her neighbor who had dropped by.

As I was doing my homework, I heard my grandmother's friend say, "Miss Lela, Evelena certainly does have dark skin." A bit startled at this turn in the conversation, I sat quietly with my head in a book and my heart in my throat. I waited for Grandmother's response.

What she said was, "Well, she doesn't get it from our family. It must come from the Eppses." The knot in my chest felt big and hard. Was Grandmother saying that no one in her family (or that of Granddaddy Smith) had dark skin? Did she not like my brown skin? Was she ashamed of me, or what? I wasn't quite sure what she meant, but for whatever reason, I felt a sense of betrayal.

All I know with certainty is that whether it was right or wrong, justified or not, the small seeds of suspicion and fear about skin color that my neighbor had planted a year or so earlier received a heavy dose of fertilizer that afternoon. The seeds of suspicion and fear hadn't grown rapidly, nor did they threaten to overtake my overall sense of self-worth. Instead, those two seeds of doubt and concern about my brown skin color became wild weeds that appeared sometimes as an unexpected, unwanted, and ugly blemish on the landscape of my usually self-assured self. This was one of those times.

Aside from a few off-the-wall remarks such as those by our neighbor and Grandmother Smith, my heart was happy in its brown-skinned body. I knew that others seemed to live happily with their dark-brown skin. My Granddaddy Epps, with his dark-pecan coloring, was widely loved and respected, as were any number of people I knew at school, church, and in my community. That was proof enough for me that most Indian people, at least those in my little world, thought brown skin was just fine.

When I was in the eleventh grade and having Sunday dinner at the home of my godparents, the Reverend and Mrs. S. A. Hammonds Sr., a beauty contest that had been held the night before in Pembroke was the topic of conversation. Some of my godparents' relatives were also present and had attended the event.

A woman told us who'd won the contest and then described the young woman this way: "With that beautiful black hair, those very blue eyes, and that milky white skin, the other girls just didn't have a chance. She looked just like a white girl. In fact, she's as pretty as any white girl I've ever seen."

No one questioned the validity of that statement nor asked for an explanation; a couple of folks expressed their agreement. I thought about the description of the newly crowned beauty queen as we ate lunch and as the others discussed different topics.

That young woman was beautiful. I had seen her many times. But this was the first time I'd really thought about the possibility that all beauty queens had to have white skin. I never considered the idea that colored people would have beauty contests. In fact, I'd never thought about beauty contests at all; there was no need to. I knew I wasn't beautiful, and even if I were, I didn't think I'd want to get up in front of a group of people and have them staring at me.

But the comment about the new beauty queen having white skin and being as pretty as any white girl caused me to wonder. Were only white girls, or those Indian girls and women with pale skin and pretty faces, considered beautiful? I just didn't know. But I really didn't think so.

What mattered to me was this. I wanted to be accepted, without hearing any negative comments, as an Indian girl with dark-brown skin. Nothing more, nothing less.

One day when I was a senior in high school, I sat in my mother's car in Lumberton and waited for her to return from shopping. I watched people of white, black, and Indian heritages walk by, and I mentally decided if the women were pretty, passable, or ugly in appearance. Several women who were white, black, and Indian fit into my three categories of attractiveness. Then, for whatever reason, I decided to look at my face in the rear-view mirror.

Staring hard at the face that apparently was mine, I analyzed each feature as if I were a beauty expert. The brown eyes were definitely an asset, I decided, even though my brothers called them "saucer-pan eyes" (because of their size, I guessed). The skin was smooth and without blemishes and really was a nice shade of dark brown, I thought, despite some comments I'd heard to the contrary. I added skin to the asset list. The eyebrows seemed to fit the eyes and the shape of the head rather well, but that was no big thing, so that didn't count either way. The full lips were questionable; some might associate them with colored people, based on comments I'd heard, while others might think they're inviting. I decided that one plus and one minus equaled zero for the lips.

Put it all together, and the outcome was what? Not beautiful, not pretty, not ugly. "Attractive" might be too strong, and "cute" didn't seem to fit. So what was the description? As if right on cue, "presentable" came out of the blue.

Suddenly, I wondered if having white skin would make a difference in how I looked. Would I be more attractive? I peered into the mirror and mentally tried to erase all the brownness from my face. I found it virtually impossible to do so. When I erased the brown from one spot, I could tell that it was still nearby. With much concentration, I continued my mental removal of brown face color. It didn't take much time for me to break out in laughter. Me with a white face? That was absurd! I looked weird and unnatural. I was foreign to myself. I knew once and for all that God had created me just the way I was supposed to be, starting with dark-brown skin.

No mirrors were thrown out when I was a senior in high school; I often looked to make sure I was presentable. Most of the time, I believed I passed that test. Without realizing it, I had not only comprehended what my parents' views about beauty and appearance really meant, but any concern that I personally had about the value of my brown skin also disappeared.

My realization that no one could define who and what I was based on the color of my skin was a huge step into young adulthood. *I was me.* And I liked myself just the way I was. Now my big hope was that some well-mannered and handsome boys out there would like me as I was and that they would call me soon.

⌒

Of course, the issue of skin color didn't end in the twelfth grade, just as it hadn't begun then. I knew, without knowing, that others would likely use my skin color as a weapon of torment in the future. I also knew that I would recognize the absurdity of such intents and the ignorance of the troublemakers. I believed that I would be OK with whatever came my way.

Sometimes when I heard people describe someone as being pretty or beautiful, I would look carefully. A few Indian girls who had olive or light-brown skin were in the pretty or beautiful category, but the majority of the ones they singled out had fair skin.

I remembered the conversation about the Indian beauty queen who "looked just like a white girl." And one day my thoughts turned to the Lumbee Indians, my mother's people.

The Lumbees are a large group of Indian people; they are the largest group of American Indians east of the Mississippi. Our appearances vary widely, especially our skin colors, which range from pale to dark. Our physical features include characteristics often associated with each of the three groups of people living in Robeson County: Indians, blacks, and whites. None of this was surprising to me, given the likelihood that Lumbees had intermingled and intermarried with both white and black people for generations. All of us—whether pale or dark skinned, thick or thin lipped, blue or brown eyed (or another combination), or with heads topped with straight, curly, or wavy hair—were Lumbee Indians. That's what my parents told me.

This kind of thinking was the basis for agreement, disagreement, pride, denials, fights, and taunts, depending on the beliefs of individuals and families. In my immediate family, we accepted this thinking as fact, which left no room for disparaging or demeaning comments about other Indian people by young or old members of the household or by visitors.

Even though I was taught to accept a variety of Lumbee appearances, I believed that the Lumbee Indian community had a certain standard of beauty, most often unspoken, that generally set white-looking appearances over dark ones. This, I thought, was especially true with any characteristic that was more closely associated with blackness.

What I came to believe was quite simple. Many of the Lumbee people I grew up with, including some of my relatives, adopted the white standard of beauty as their own. Perhaps doing so wasn't conscious or intentional, but it was the reality that I saw. It was, I expect, this kind of thinking that triggered my neighbor's warnings about her son and me getting "too dark." At worst it was prejudice masqueraded as neighborliness; at best it was an act of protection from what she knew to be true or believed to be fact. Perhaps my grandmother's response about my dark skin came from this vantage as well. Or maybe I misinterpreted her comment.

Another facet of skin color troubled me more than what I perceived as Indians using white beauty as the standard of beauty for our people. This concern was how many of the Indian children and adults I knew viewed "colored people." Surely, no one in the world was talked about with as much degradation as colored people. What I heard at school, and in some conversations in the community, was simply hateful. Many of the derogatory comments focused on behaviors, which I found puzzling, since I believed anyone of any color could act in a way that people described as "acting like a nigger."

Some of my classmates throughout elementary and high school used comments about colored people's physical characteristics to demean other Indian students: "Aw, shut up, you nigger lips. You don't know what you're talking about." This was an insult that usually produced a scuffle or fight.

My classmates and close relatives frequently talked about hair with straight and slight waves being preferred over hair with too many curls. Actually, curly hair was acceptable. It was tightly curled, coarse hair that was referred to as "kinky" or "bad" hair. Neither was desirable, I learned. And I'll admit it: I was very glad to have very straight dark-brown hair.

In addition to hair being classified by its characteristics as either good or bad, the matter of learning sometimes became involved with hair. "Look at him with his kinky head," people would say. "You know kinky heads don't know nothing." This kind of comment was the basis for engaging in self-defense, sometimes in verbal exchanges but most often in physical encounters at recess. Not only was this person's hair less than satisfactory; it seemed that the real message was that colored people were not intelligent.

Much of what I heard didn't make sense to me; people couldn't choose or change their skin color, hair texture, or the shape of their lips. And, while those conversations made me feel uncomfortable, I listened and made no comments. But there was one thing I did know about all this talk of skin, hair, lips, behaviors, and intelligence: my parents would not approve of the insults and bad language anyone used to describe other human beings.

⁓

From the time I was a preteen, I became aware of the appearance of my relatives and other people in the High Plains community, where my dad was born and spent his childhood. The appearances of Indians there included a variety of skin colors, hair textures, and lip sizes. Some people's physical characteristics resembled those of white people, and some people's skin was pecan brown, like Granddaddy Epps's and mine. A few people's hair texture was more similar to that of black people. But to me, the majority of those living in the High Plains community had a similar look: medium olive or tan skin, dark eyes, straight dark or black hair, and lips that ranged from thin to full.

What set the High Plains Indian community apart from many of my Saddletree neighbors, a few of my relatives, and other Lumbees I knew was that I never heard anyone, young or old, speak in negative or demeaning language about anyone's appearance. Nor did I hear comparisons to other races in terms of beauty or behavioral characteristics. Perhaps I wasn't there long enough or often enough to hear this kind of talk, or maybe the adults discussed it when I wasn't around. But since I heard no conversations, or even bits of ones, that used racial characteristics as belittling or demeaning, it made a lasting impression on me. I believed that the High Plains Indians accepted the appearance of people without judgment.

Were the High Plains Indians more comfortable with their appearance than some of the Lumbees? I didn't know. But it was a welcome change not to hear words that made me cringe and then feel guilty because I hadn't said anything about mean comments about black people. I was especially grateful that I never heard any disparaging comments about my own appearance.

Inever knew with certainty why my father's and mother's people differed so greatly on what I perceived as the preferred look of beauty. But this I did know after sixteen years of being an Indian girl with dark-brown skin: I was glad that my mother lived by the credo that pretty is as pretty does.

With much practice on my behavior and some time spent in front of the mirror to make sure my body was clean and my hair and clothes were in place, I was fairly certain that my look would be *presentable*. That's what I hoped—then and now.

Awareness-Photographs

Noyal Ann Hunt (left) and Lena, sixth grade

Lena, seventh grade

Franklin, Mama, Daddy, Cam, and Lena, eighth grade

Community Life

Saints and Sinners

The building sat at the edge of Ten Mile Swamp, where vines and trees competed for growing space, dark waters pooled, and animals of the wet and wild were said to live. To the rear were fields with rich soils that produced crops, hard work, and the hope of enough money to make ends meet for those who farmed them. On the opposite side from the murky swamp was the hushed stillness and eerie quiet that is found only in cemeteries. Cars and trucks rushed by on Highway 301, at the building's front border. Many people who saw this place from a distance were unaware that this was a place of simple goodness and great importance to many. This was Ten Mile Center Baptist Church.

Originally, the church was a simple square white-frame building, but with time it faded into pale gray. One or more of the windows seemed to always have a cracked pane; panes were often broken or completely missing. Vandals had no sense of right or wrong. At the rear of the building, on both sides, small wings opened to the outside, with a single door providing access to the sandy ground that was the foundation for the building. A small steeple with a bell adorned its top. Unlike the rest of the building, the steeple was safe from late-night visitors except for the pigeons that often used it as home.

Not far away from the church was an in-ground hand pump that provided drinking water for all who wanted any. At a safe distance from the pump, near the back field, a crude wooden outhouse served as the toilet for women and girls; the men's facility, similar in construction, stood closer to the swamp. Both the pump and the men's toilet were a very respectable distance away from the female facility.

Ten Mile Center Baptist Church was nothing much to look at on the outside. Even the yard looked somewhat neglected. There were no blooming flowers, well-trimmed shrubs, or manicured lawn. The yard was sandy and had little grass. What it did have was plenty of sandspurs that latched onto socks and trousers. All too often, they also attached themselves to human skin, especially that of ladies with nylon stockings and little girls with bare legs.

One entered the church through double front doors that never seemed to stay closed completely. Any efforts to repair the doors' lock never lasted long. The old people of the church were solemn as they told the children that "haints" (the Lumbee word for haunt—a spirit or ghost) walked in and out of the church. That's why the church doors never stayed closed. Little children listened in silence and watched the doors closely. Some things weren't meant to be discussed.

Once past the double doors that were opened and closed by the haints, the church had little to see that was visually appealing, and certainly nothing awe inspiring. Handmade benches served as seating for the faithful and for guests. Constructed of a 2 x 4 frame, the bottom and back of each bench consisted of slats of 1 x 4 lumber spaced about four inches apart. There were no cushions to keep the slats on the hard benches from pinching or gouging. For those of us who weren't yet adults or those who had little body fat, the pews pinched our lower body parts. Sitting for more than five minutes could be painful, but physical comfort wasn't the issue of concern. This was the Lord's house; the issue of concern was having a right relationship with the Lord Jesus Christ. No more, no less, no matter the age!

Benches lined both sides of the room, with a center aisle that served as the passageway for getting to other parts of the church. One could walk straight ahead to the altar and pulpit or take a right or left to the Sunday school classrooms located on either side. In the main sanctuary, a large wood-burning stove provided heat in the cold of winter. To the left of the stove, a desk waited for the Sunday school superintendent to perform his administrative duties, such as making announcements and rendering a call to attend prayer meetings on Wednesday nights. On the right-front wall was an ancient piano that sounded out of tune much of the time. Far in the back of the room, in a corner, a rope dangled that was connected to the bell in the steeple.

Ten Mile Center Baptist Church was where my family attended church. It was sometimes confused with the Barker Ten Mile Church, located a few miles away. To those of us who went to the church on Highway 301, however, ours was the *real* Ten Mile Church. It was the church where Indians worshipped; the other one had a white congregation. The two churches probably had other differences, but we really didn't know.

The congregation at Ten Mile was small. On a really good Sunday, a hundred people were present. This occurred at homecoming, Easter, or near Christmas and was announced with great satisfaction. Average attendance was more likely to number forty to fifty people, including both adults and children. On some Sundays, the faithful dwindled to twenty-five. Most of the people who attended were from the Saddletree community, although some people came from the Antioch community and as far away as Lumberton and St. Pauls.

Sunday worship officially began at 10a.m. The call to worship was the ringing of the church bell; often, startled pigeons flew out as the bell pealed. Everyone gathered in the main room of the church, and the service started. If we were there on time, then the Sunday school superintendent (my father) welcomed all to the service. My mother played the piano as the faithful saints and sinners sang their favorite hymns. No hymnbooks were needed for "Rescue the Perishing," "Trust and Obey," "Standing on the Promises," and a multitude of other old gospel favorites. If we weren't on time, then Mr. Seymour Bell led the service without hesitation or piano music.

Mr. Seymour Bell was short, had very little hair, and was in his seventies. He often walked five miles to church. Unless a driving rain or frigid cold delayed him, he arrived long before we or anyone else did. Once it was ten o'clock, he pulled the rope in the back of the church, and the bell began to ring. Mr. Seymour was known to say, "Let's start on time and let's end on time. It's time to worship the Lord."

Mr. Seymour led the congregation from where he sat on the left front of the room. Depending on how The Spirit led him, he would lead the congregation in one song. Or we might sing three or four. He used no hymnbook. The words to the songs were etched in his heart and were at the tip of his tongue. He offered prayers of thanksgiving for the Lord's Day that touched all hearts, even those who hated long prayers. The opening service Mr. Seymour conducted was never quite as short as when Daddy or one of the other male church members officiated. He was the elder, and it was his privilege to lead as he was led by the Holy Spirit. No one thought otherwise.

Praising God with song was important at Ten Mile Center. Though none us had trained singing voices, our little congregation sang with great fervor and loud voices. Often, we sang with no real attention to the cadence of the piano accompaniment. Neither the faithful nor the pianist seemed to notice. Our song leader, Miss Eunice (Mrs. Eunice Hammonds), and later Miss Sue (Mrs. Sue Jones), seemed not to notice that we were often out of synch. (As I mentioned earlier, all women were "Miss" whether they were single or married.) The fact that we were "making a joyful noise" was enough.

Our congregational group singing was the appetizer of the day. We were warming up, getting ourselves in the right frame of mind for the main event, which was Sunday School. We would be fed spiritually, whether we were hungry or not.

After the short praise and praying session, everyone except the adults went to a room in the two little side wings for Sunday School. The particular room each person attended was based on his or her age. Classes and activities for the youngest who attended Sunday School were held in the right wing of the building. The mothers of babies and toddlers took them to the nursery, where Miss Stella (Mrs. Stella Bell) cared for them with a grandmotherly eye. The soft-spoken Miss Lela (Mrs. Lela Hunt) taught the "primaries": young children who were between the ages of four and seven. Children from eight to twelve received instruction from the vivacious Miss Vernie (Mrs. Vernie Chavis), the junior class teacher.

Older children, those of middle and high school age and beyond, went to the left wing and were instructed by Miss Maude (Mrs. Maude Revels), the mild-mannered teacher of the intermediate class. The challenge of holding the attention of young adults belonged to Miss Eunice, an insightful woman who knew what we faced outside the church and didn't mince any words about how we should respond to worldly pitfalls and pressures. Adults remained in the main room of the church and were taught by my mother.

For forty-five minutes, we heard serious instructions on how to live based on Bible teachings. The teachers were women who took their Christian responsibility seriously. They were prepared in both scriptural background and in understanding child and adult learning styles.

When I was in the junior class, Miss Vernie tried to make sure that we all understood the point of her lessons. She asked direct questions and expected answers that reflected righteous thinking. Often, the responses she received were likely not what she hoped for or wished to hear. "Now, Evelena, what is Jesus trying to teach us in this story?" Miss Vernie asked me once.

"To live by the Golden Rule," I answered.

"And what does that mean?"

Miss Vernie's students knew that the Golden Rule was the best way, but we were worldly enough to know that, sometimes, this just didn't seem to make the most sense. So we would try to persuade our gentle teacher that occasionally other people didn't deserve that kind of treatment.

"It doesn't matter what they say or do. You are Christian boys and girls. You have to set the example. *You should do what Jesus would do*," she would say. Miss Vernie summarized the lesson and the role of Christians in a non-Christian world in four sentences. She'd won again. We knew just enough to understand that this was the final answer. Whether we liked it or not, the discussion was over.

Years later, when we were young adults and Miss Eunice was our teacher, she taught us about the ways of Satan and temptations. She often used herself and her family as examples. "Satan doesn't want you to come to church on Sundays. He doesn't want me to be here, either," she said. "When I woke up this morning, I heard a little voice speaking to me. And the little voice spoke these words: 'I know you don't feel well this morning. Why don't you just sleep in? You'd feel so much better.' That, young people, is the Devil," Miss Eunice proclaimed. "That is *temptation*. Don't *fall for it*."

Miss Eunice made her point with me. If she, a devoted Christian, faced temptation on a regular basis, then I was in for some trouble. I expected to be tempted. And I expected to fail the test. Being a young adult meant having fun, trying things out, and occasionally lying to cover one's wrong ways to parents who disapproved of much of what I thought was attractive and fun.

This living for Jesus was going to make my life hard. I wasn't so sure that I wanted to hear more. Miss Eunice understood all that. But she never wavered in her call for us to be on guard against the temptations she knew were waiting outside of Ten Mile Center Baptist Church.

The message of our Sunday school teachers was forcefully endorsed on the two Sundays of the month when we had preaching at eleven following Sunday school. We sang, we prayed, and we gave our offerings and tithes. But the most important thing on those two Sundays was that we listened to preaching that left nothing to the imagination about the importance of living right.

Our preachers were men, most often Indian men, called by God to deliver His message. They always started with at least one selection of Bible reading, which then served as the basis for the message of the day. No matter what the selection, the Bible we used was the King James Version. There was no other, as far as we knew. No matter what verse or chapter or whether it was the Old or New Testament, every word was true. Everyone knew that.

From the first word of the Scripture reading to the final word of the sermon, what was said was Spirit led. What this meant was that there were no notes, no outline, and no written sermon. At least I never saw any. The preacher said what God had "on his heart," and he did so with a voice that ranged from a whisper to a shout. Often, he emphasized an important point with an upraised hand holding a Bible. Sometimes the preacher made his point with his hand, which hit the pulpit with such force that little ones sat up straight to see what exactly was going on.

A few of our preachers delivered their sermons in a low-key manner that was characterized by a teaching approach and a conversational-style voice. Most of our preachers delivered their sermons in a style my brothers and I called "Indian style." While both styles of preaching began with a normal vocal tone, the Indian-style preachers' voices increased in volume as the preacher made key points. What I perceived as the signature mark of our Indian preachers who were "on fire for the Lord" was the insertion of what sounded like the word "Ha," coupled with a gasping for a breath of air between certain key phrases. One knew that the preacher was going full force when that occurred.

Most of the sermons had certain common themes: temptation, damnation, and salvation. Often, all three were present in a single sermon. When this happened, the atmosphere of the church became electric. The Holy Spirit was at work. Sunday dinner would not come anytime soon.

An example of a portion of the sermon where the preacher was "on fire with the Spirit" would be something like this: "It's easy to go along with the crowd: Ha! Go drinking, run with the unsaved, and live it up. Ha! That's what old Satan wants you to do. Ha! But it's not what Jesus wants. Ha!"

Often, when the preacher was delivering his message with intensity, an adult would utter an amen. Most of the time, the response of the adults was a nod from the head and a supporting "yes!" But that was not my response.

I watched the preacher with a mixture of curiosity and concern. Many times I became alarmed as I watched the preacher's face change from his usual color of tan or brown to one that had a decidedly red tint. My concern was that something dreadful would happen to him right there in the pulpit. Would he pass out, have a stroke, or experience some other medical emergency? Would he die in the pulpit? What would we do if something happened as he was proclaiming the Word?

I had no reason to continue with this silent questioning and persistent concern, since I knew the preacher's style would remain the same. My real issue was that loud voices in communication unnerved me. I always focused on the sound more than the subject when the volume of someone's voice went up. And I knew that I would not receive much, if any, sympathy from my mother when I complained to her.

"Lena, how the preacher preaches isn't what's important; it's what he says that matters. Listen and you'll learn something you need to know. Then, put it into practice."

It was wise advice, but I often didn't heed it.

Meanwhile, as the preacher preached on, children of all ages were aware that one or more purplish/silver/blue little creatures that we called purple scorpions (actually southeastern skinks) were walking across the walls behind the pulpit. We watched with fascination as they scampered from one wall to the other. We watched with wonder that the preacher seemed unaware of them or chose to ignore their presence.

I watched with fear, hoping that the ugly little things wouldn't decide to come and visit those of us sitting on the hard benches. For no matter how much Mama had told us to sit up and behave, I would head for the nearest door if a purple scorpion left the pulpit area and appeared to be coming anywhere near me. Whatever punishment I would receive was nothing compared to my fear of the purple scorpions. After all, we'd been warned that these scorpions were capable of delivering a "deadly sting" to humans. It was much later that we learned that this was a myth.

Never losing a breath or a word because of the scorpions, the preacher continued: "You must be born again! Ha! It is the only way to get to heaven. Ha! Don't think that good works will get you there. Ha! That kind of thinking will get you to the burning fires of hell. Ha! Think about it: Where do you want to spend eternity? Ha! Come to Jesus now while you still have the chance."

This would continue until the preacher had made his main points and he was ready to extend an invitation to all sinners to accept Jesus Christ as their savior. Sometimes it seemed to take an awfully long time to get to the invitation portion of the service.

A hymn of invitation—most often hymn number 100 in the *Broadman Hymnal*, "Softly and Tenderly"—urged us to "come home." Prayers and exhortations for sinners to make a confession of their sins and to accept Jesus were said as the congregation sang. Most Sundays the invitation went unanswered, but sometimes a sinner made a decision to live for Christ. The sinner who chose to ask God to forgive him or her and to accept Jesus as savior was met at the altar by the preacher and other saints of the church. Prayers of thanksgiving for the sinner's repentance were offered with great feeling. Often prayers of guidance for everyone present, especially the new convert, were lifted up as well. Together, on bended knee and in love of Jesus, a sinner became a saint. This new saint became one in Christ with the old saints of the church. They were at home in God's house on Highway 301 north, Ten Mile Center Baptist Church. The rejoicing was real.

After the service ended, children of all ages played on the church grounds; some of the braver ones ventured into the cemetery. My personal goal was to avoid the cemetery at all costs but to do so without betraying my profound fear of walking near the graves. After all, some of the graves had become sinkholes in the sandy soil. Some of the older children, mostly boys, claimed that caskets were visible without any trouble at all. One older boy declared that another boy had seen part of a skeleton when he looked into the sandy hole. *I had no desire* to see any portion of a casket or whatever else might be below the surface of the ground in a cemetery. I left the cemetery activities to my fearless brothers.

Hanging around on the church ground following the preaching, the adults talked about the usual things: health, weather, crops, and sometimes the sermon. "The preacher really laid it on us," one older man said. Nodding heads affirmed his statement. That was a compliment of the highest order. The churchgoers had heard what the preacher had said. They recognized an applicable truth in the sermon. It remained to be seen if the message would have an impact beyond Sunday. Some adults said it was spiritual nourishment for the coming week. A small group of saints would return for the Wednesday-evening prayer service and pray for those sinners who still ignored the call of God and the local preacher.

For the little ones and young people, we were glad it was Sunday. We had escaped our chores and schoolwork. We were glad that Jesus loved us, and we enjoyed the singing. But right now, we were glad to be going home so that we could change into casual clothes and have Sunday dinner. After all, saints and sinners had to eat. And both saints and sinners knew that Sunday dinner was a heavenly feast.

The Politics of Fried Fish

Politics and food went together as naturally in eastern North Carolina as the rice and gravy my mother used to cook for Sunday dinner. For some, the food associated with politics was chicken; for others, the choice of meat for a political gathering was barbecue. Of course, they were talking about barbecue made from hog meat; in Saddletree, it was simply called "Q."

Surprisingly, my introduction to politics included neither Q nor chicken. There was no organized gathering of officials or even "wanna-be" candidates. My entry into the mysteries of politics came by way of the church, and the food of choice was fried fish.

The highlight of many Sundays in my early youth was to have dinner with Miss Hammonds. Though we called her that, she was Mrs. Sarah Margaret Hammonds, the wife of the Rev. Steven A. Hammonds Sr. They were the respected matriarch and patriarch of a prominent Indian family in the Saddletree community. Their landholdings were considerable, and they operated a small general store, known as the Commissary, located on the edge of their front yard facing Rennert Road.

The Hammondses' home was the largest and nicest home I'd ever visited. Constructed of bricks, it was spacious and even had an indoor bathroom. The living and dining rooms were furnished unlike any I had ever seen. My mother called it "formal mahogany"—whatever that meant. I knew that it meant do not touch any of the little "sit-arounds" (small items that seemed to serve no function other than ashtrays) that were on end tables and larger pieces of furniture. It also meant "do not bump into any furniture." What impressed me even more than the house or furniture was the shiny Buick parked in the carport adjacent to the front porch. It always looked new.

Though Miss Hammonds and her husband were older than my parents, their friendship was one of long standing, great respect, and deep affection for each other. Miss Hammonds was known as a woman of deep religious convictions, a love of fishing, and her amazing abilities as a cook. She, too, was a faithful member of Ten Mile Center Baptist Church.

An invitation to eat Sunday dinner at the Hammondses' home rarely was extended ahead of time. Usually, Miss Hammonds would approach my mother after church. "Miss Grace," she would ask, "why don't you and Mr. Epps and the children come home with me and eat dinner?"

"I think that would be fine. Let me talk to Frank for a minute," my mother usually responded.

We knew that we would have a banquet of a meal. At the top of the list of foods that made our mouths water and our stomachs growl just thinking about it was fried fish. I remember perch, and my brothers remember pike. Our hostess caught both in the dark waters of the Saddletree Swamp near her home and the Ten Mile Swamp next to the church.

"There will be no running through the house, no name-calling, and no fighting or fussing. Do you understand?" Mama's speech was a familiar one, and she had little time to remind us of what she expected of us as we rode the short distance from the church to our Sunday dinner destination. "Do not touch or lift anything in the living room. I mean *anything*. Do you hear me?"

The three voices of her dear children, whose behavior never quite measured up to her efforts at teaching them proper manners, replied in unison, "Yes, Mama, we hear."

Upon arriving at the Hammondses' home, we'd greet whoever else was there besides Miss Hammonds and her husband, Preacher Steve. Usually, this meant at least one adult child of the Hammonds family and some of their children. It didn't take long for all the young children to be told to leave the kitchen and dining room. The women had serious work to do.

My brothers and I always raced to the front porch first. We called it "walking fast." Our mother and dad called it running. "Slow down, now," my dad said as we "walked" very quickly past where he and the other men sat. We reached an inviting swing on the front porch before he could finish his sentence.

As always, the porch swing generated chaos. Instead of the swing soothing us with its gentle rocking motion, my brothers and I squabbled about who had more sitting space and how fast the swing should go. I always dutifully reported to Mama that I had been unable to settle this controversy. Soon she would appear on the porch.

"Go see the fish," she said to Franklin and Cam.

My brothers loved that instruction. At the Hammondses' home, children and adults alike marveled at the sight of a small, circular, concrete fishpond in the front yard. It contained a variety of fish and plants.

"Look at that one!" Franklin shouted. "He's really big!"

Without a pause, Cam replied, "Let's catch him."

They leaned forward and stuck their four- and five-year-old hands into the dark waters of the pond. Laughing loudly, Brother exclaimed, "It got away, you get him!"

I knew it was time to notify our mother once again of the unapproved outdoor activities of "the boys," the description my dad used often when talking about Brother and Cam.

With the Epps children's behavior under control, the women completed the familiar routine of finishing Sunday dinner. Miss Hammonds fried platters of fish. Miss Mary or Miss Eunice produced dozens of hush puppies, and my mother finished setting the tables and set out the previously prepared vegetables. The men continued to sit and talk.

Sometimes, I walked quietly into the dining room as we waited for the call for dinner. I marveled at an entire wall of built-in cabinets full of china and crystal. The table easily seated ten, and the tablecloth was much too beautiful for crumbs and gravy drippings to touch it.

I knew it was almost time to eat when I heard Miss Hammonds say it was time to fix punch for the children. My brothers and I loved the children's punch, as everyone called it. Miss Hammonds poured bottles of RC Cola, Nehi Grape, and Orange Crush soft drinks—all from their store—into a large metal pitcher. She added some water, a bit of sugar, and a handful of ice cubes and stirred. It was always delicious. Only Miss Hammonds made it.

As the grown-ups seated themselves at the large mahogany dining room table covered with a cutwork, damask, or lace tablecloth, the young children's plates were served on a bare table in the kitchen.

"Don't eat a bite until after the blessing is said," we were instructed.

It was a command that fell on mostly deaf ears.

By the time I was in the sixth grade, I was allowed to eat with the adults and infrequent guests of high school or college age. Oh, I was so proud! I recognized this as a privilege, even though I was unsure of the criteria for this honor. Out of my mother's earshot, I told my brothers it was because I knew how to behave and had grown-up table manners. They always laughed and said they didn't care.

Preacher Steve sat at the head of the table and offered a prayer of thanks for the food. In true Southern Baptist tradition, his prayer seemed to go on forever. Finally, the platters and bowls of food were passed. Vegetables seasoned with animal fat of some type made even peas taste delicious. Who could not love boiled potatoes with a film of real butter coating every bite? Dinner always featured a huge bowl of tangy coleslaw. Dozens of fish fried to golden-brown perfection were piled high on a platter, and the smell of hot hush puppies always reached one's nose before the basket arrived from the left. The Lord and I both knew we had plenty to give thanks for on these days.

It was at this Sunday dinner table of my godparents, Preacher Steve and Miss Hammonds, that my interest in and recognition of the importance of politics really began. No matter what the office or who the candidate was, the fried-fish political forum focused on Democratic politics. The exception was a presidential election. The political talk usually began when Daddy turned to Mr. Harry West Locklear, an in-law of the host family, and asked, "What's going on in Pembroke?"

"Things are looking good," Mr. Locklear would reply. Then the visiting political observer would say something like, "Looks like the Democrats will make a clean sweep on the state level, but I don't know about the presidential election. I think that Pembroke will go for Stevenson, but there's a lot of support for Ike."

Even I knew that General Eisenhower was a national hero. I'd heard comments about how "he got our boys back home from the war." I waited for Daddy's response.

"We'll see how it comes out," he would usually say.

The conversation about the presidential race stopped then, but I remembered Daddy had told me that he thought Stevenson was the best of all the presidential candidates. "I think he's too smart for the average voter," he'd told me earlier, "but I'm going to vote for him anyway."

I hoped that Mr. Stevenson would win, because I believed that my dad's choice would certainly be the best one.

At the time, the Democratic primary races for statewide offices were intense. The campaign to become the Democratic nominee for governor was particularly hard fought. A family friend put it this way: "They say whoever wins that Democratic primary will be the next governor. There's not enough Republicans in the whole state of North Carolina to even bother with the November election."

Sometimes the Pembroke and Saddletree residents at the dinner table supported different candidates for governor. It was, I thought, because the Pembroke guests were "town people," and we were "country people." I learned that disagreements on which gubernatorial candidate would best serve Indian needs didn't keep this group from agreement on one point. Everyone was unanimous in their belief that the state political system needed to do more than talk and to do more than it had in the past for Indian education in Robeson County.

In 1952 the Democratic nominee for governor was William B. Umstead, a well-qualified man according to the conversation at the fried fish dinner political discussion. The point at which the political conversation about the governor's race got really interesting was when the topics of education and roads came up. More people expressed their opinions, and the voices around the table sounded more passionate than usual. A governor could affect issues and concerns on the local level. The lives of Indians could be affected in a positive or negative manner.

"I read that Umstead promised to fight for education funds," Miss Mary said. A first-grade teacher, she was the wife of Mr. Harry West.

"The Lord knows we need that in Robeson County," Mama said. "There's always a shortage of books."

Then Daddy spoke. "Everybody knows the roads need attention. It's a wonder some of our school buses can even get close to some of the students' homes. It's a shame how far some of our students have to walk to get to the bus." He spoke with a quiet firmness that no one questioned because he had the responsibility of developing the bus routes for Magnolia School. The conversation invariably lingered on education; its importance to Indian people, especially, was a recurrent theme.

Sometimes we were eating third helpings of fried fish and hush puppies when the next round of political talk started. This was usually the liveliest and longest of the conversations about elections. I knew before it began that it would focus on Robeson County politics.

"Who's going to win the sheriff's race?" my dad asked.

"Looks like McLeod has it locked up," someone replied as I tried to eat, have good table manners, and listen all at the same time.

"Well, Saddletree will turn out to vote, and the candidates know that, too. We all know that's a good thing." That was a pronouncement from Miss Hammonds I didn't understand. I did understand that it wasn't polite to ask questions; my job was to eat and behave. And I surely wasn't going to risk public reproach by my parents on this point. No one else asked or commented about what she'd said. So either they understood, or they knew better than to question the matriarch in her home.

By this time, the younger children at the kitchen table had long finished their dinner. They had also used up their Sunday quota of good manners.

"Mama, come get Cam!" Brother Franklin said loudly.

Laughter and loud noises summoned Mama and one other woman to check on the children.

"Miss Grace, go ahead and give the children some dessert," our kind hostess said. "Then, they can go out and play."

For a few seconds, I was sorry I wasn't in the kitchen with my brothers and the other children. I was ready for dessert, too.

If the entire truth were told, I was always ready for dessert before I arrived. The fried fish, hush puppies, and punch were really good—delicious in fact. The talk about who might be our next president, governor, or sheriff was interesting. I paid extremely close attention to the talk about the sheriff. According to neighbors and church friends, people needed to know his name and, if possible, someone who knew him well. The sheriff was described as "the law" in my community. No further explanation was given or needed. When I heard adults say that the sheriff was the most powerful person in the county, I believed them.

Right now, however, I looked forward to what I knew was coming next: pound cake and talk about the local school politics.

"What do you hear about the board race?" It was Daddy who asked the question.

I knew with certainty that "the board" was the Robeson County Board of Education. Everyone employed by the Robeson County schools in any way understood the significance of the board members, and several people at the dinner table were teachers or school staff.

The board of education developed policies and made rules for all the county schools, and the board allocated funds for all the county schools: white, black, and Indian. They had final approval of who was hired to teach. But in my child's eyes, it seemed that their most important function was the appointment of local school committee board members.

Various people shared the news they'd heard from Pembroke and Saddletree about who was likely to win or retain a seat on the board of education. "The boys in Lumberton; that's another story," Mr. Locklear said.

Some of the adults talked about how they thought Lumberton residents would vote for board candidates. "You know Lumberton doesn't want us to have anything," said a voice I recognized as belonging to Miss Mary.

"Amen to that," proclaimed Miss Eunice, and that part of the conversation ended.

Everyone agreed that the attitude of the county board of education toward Indians was mostly pathetically poor. All the members of the county school board were white, and few, if any, genuinely cared about Indian students. It was a reality that was unlikely to change anytime soon.

One of the Pembroke guests spoke very clearly: "The superintendent and his staff aren't any better."

"Well, I don't know about that," Daddy said. "The superintendent can only work with what he has. He treats me fairly. But I agree that he's got some folks who could do a lot better."

I digested these words carefully, for it was rare that he spoke openly about his employer.

"The day will come," Mama said, "when things will get better. It's got to get better. I just hope and pray it won't be too long."

As regular as clockwork, the adults' talk then returned to the importance of education for Indian children. Miss Mary talked about her first-grade students and said, "It's hard to learn if someone doesn't help them at home."

My mother bemoaned the fact that Indian students missed far too many days of school. Preacher Steve and my dad talked about the impact that farming had on families.

"Parents need their children to work in the fields, but the children need a good education," Preacher Steve said.

Heads nodded silently in agreement.

My stomach was more than full, and I was more than tired of "being nice." Miss Hammonds had obviously noticed the look of boredom on my face. Maybe she caught my bony body in its fidgety mode. "Miss Grace," she said, "tell Evelena to take her plate and glass to the kitchen and then go sit on the porch."

My mother didn't have to repeat my godmother's directive twice. I left without saying a word.

The front porch of the Hammondses' home covered the width of the house. There were two sets of double-hung windows on either side of the front door. One set was very near the porch swing, which made it very convenient to hear what was being said inside the living room if the windows were open. I learned at a very early age that the swing was often the very best spot for hearing news that adults didn't discuss in the presence of children.

After the men finished eating, they were invited to move to the living room while the women cleared the dining room table and put away the food. A beautiful sofa and equally handsome chairs provided ample seating in the dimly lit room for the men to get comfortable after such a large meal. It was also a perfect place to talk about an issue of local importance if they chose to pursue the topic.

"Mr. Epps, what's the situation with your school committee?" I could tell that it was Mr. Harry West who spoke. My ears opened wide on the porch swing when I heard the question. I wanted to make sure I heard the answer. The local school committee consisted of community residents appointed by the county board of education and were viewed by community residents as people with positions of great power. The local school committee made recommendations for the hiring and rehiring of the principal, teachers, and staff for the local school.

"Oh, I think it'll be all right," Daddy replied.

"Do you think anyone will get moved off?" asked Preacher Steve.

A brief paused followed, and then Daddy spoke: "I've heard rumors that at least one person will be replaced, but only time will tell."

"Who do you think it will be?" asked Mr. Harry West.

I sat up really straight now, for this was extremely important. This could affect my dad's job. I hoped it wasn't either of our neighbors who were members of the Magnolia School committee. I felt sure they liked my dad and would support him when it came time to vote for the principal for the coming school year.

"I don't know," my dad replied. "They all serve at the pleasure of the board, and you know that could mean anything's possible."

"Well, the folks around here are pretty well connected," Preacher Steve said, "so I'd guess it would be one of the other members."

"We'll just have to wait and see," Dad responded.

I still knew nothing definitive. Daddy didn't seem too concerned—at least not like I was. One of my classmates had alarmed me recently. Her brother had gotten into serious trouble at school, and my dad had suspended him for a week.

"My daddy's getting your dad fired," she told me on the school grounds at recess. "He's already visited the committee. It's going to be goodbye for Mr. Epps."

Maybe she was just talking. That's what I hoped, anyway.

November came, and almost immediately it was Election Day. My parents voted at the Saddletree precinct on Rennert Road. Neither of them made any comments on the turnout or possible outcome of any race.

After supper my dad turned on the radio. It was early yet, for local results for Robeson County votes were tallied by hand. He tuned into WPTF in Raleigh and listened as the commentators broadcast their predictions about North Carolina's statewide elections. Occasionally, they provided a report on the presidential race.

"How's Stevenson doing, Daddy?" I asked.

"Too early to tell, Lena. It takes a long time to count votes in every state. You'll be asleep then. You'll find out in the morning."

Later, when Mama was forcing me to go to bed, I heard Daddy tell her, "Grace, I'm going to run up to the polls to see what's going on."

"All right, but I'll be in bed when you get back," Mama replied.

This was a predictable routine on election night. I knew that whatever went on at the polls was either very interesting or very important. Daddy didn't often stay up late.

On his way to work the next morning, Daddy gave me the report on the presidential election.

"General Eisenhower will be the next president," he said.

"Well, he won't be mine. I wanted Stevenson to win," I said.

"Lena, General Eisenhower was elected by the people of this nation. He didn't win here in Robeson County. Stevenson beat him two to one, but that wasn't enough. Whether we wanted him to win or not isn't important now. He will be the president of *all* the people. That includes us." Daddy walked out the door, and I thought about how he'd emphasized the word *all*.

After the election, what most people talked about was the outcome of the local races. Most of what I heard was about Malcolm G. McLeod, who was elected sheriff. Several people voiced the opinion that Mr. McLeod's election was a good thing.

"I told them boys he'd win," Tom Burnett, a longtime family friend, said. "From now on, maybe they'll listen to me."

"Maybe they will," my dad responded. "Maybe they ought to." A smile was on his face.

"We Indians need all the help we can get in that department," said Tom. "You know how it goes sometimes."

"I believe Mr. McLeod will treat Indian people fairly," my dad said.

I filed that away for future reference. Daddy must have had a good reason for his statement. He didn't give out false hope just to be polite.

Not a word about the local committee reached my ears. There was no talk about school business at all. I assumed that whatever had happened didn't pose any threat to my dad's job. That was what really mattered most to me, as far as politics went.

The election of William Umstead as governor was generally received as good news. My parents were as shocked as other North Carolinians were when, two days after his inauguration in early January of 1953, Governor Umstead suffered a heart attack.

"Lordy, the man didn't hardly get sworn in as governor, and now he's about dead," Mrs. Stella Bell said.

"We need to hope and pray that he gets well and can do his work," Mama replied.

I wondered if politics had almost killed him. If so, that was something to remember.

*I*t was not just a childish impression that I had about the abundance of Democrats in the Saddletree community and Robeson County in 1952. While Robeson County was known as a Democratic stronghold, Saddletree was known as a Democratic entrenchment of exceptional party loyalty. Some folks referred to our community as being full of "yellow dog Democrats." A few people said that this meant a Democrat would vote for a yellow dog if it were on the ballot. I thought that was an exaggeration, but the election results from my childhood years document the strength of Saddletree as a Democratic haven.

Some said that Saddletree's Indian participation in elections was the result of strong political leaders. In the 1950s, those people who were mentioned frequently included Mr. Frank Bell, the Rev. Steve A. Hammonds Sr., and Mr. Herdmon Revels, though he didn't technically live in Saddletree. Each man owned land and operated a country store as well. While none of them held elected political office, they were reputed to have connections to the white political establishment in Lumberton, which controlled Democratic Party politics in Robeson County. Friends of my family claimed that white politicians often visited the Indian-owned stores, especially in election years.

There was random talk about the white politicians giving money to some Indian political leaders to make sure Indians remembered to vote. I thought that was extremely strange. My parents often said it was a privilege to vote and that everyone should vote. But Daddy and Mama never mentioned money in association with voting. It was common knowledge that a country store was a natural gathering place for Indian men to visit and talk. It made sense to me that they would discuss more than the price of gas and bread. Nobody paid grown-ups to sit at a store and talk about anything—I was fairly certain about that.

So engrained was the Democratic Party affiliation and loyalty in Saddletree that I didn't know a single Republican. At least I didn't know anyone who publicly acknowledged this in my childhood. Once I heard comments about a few white people who lived near Bethel Hill Church who were said to be Republicans. Some said that they were wealthy. My conclusion came quickly: Republicans were white and wealthy. No wonder I didn't know any.

I didn't know this for sure, but I came to believe that most Republicans lived "up North." No one told me that. Rather, I decided that based on what I'd heard, there really weren't any Republicans in Robeson County. That meant they must live in a faraway place. Up North seemed as far away from Robeson County as I could imagine at the time.

A framed document was hung in my Smith grandparents' living room in Pembroke. It named Granddaddy Smith postmaster in Pembroke and was signed by President Hoover, but I had no idea about how or why he'd been named postmaster. In fact, I never thought about it, and my parents never talked about it in my presence. All I knew was that it was ancient history.

It took many more years and dozens of fried-fish Sunday dinners to change my mind about who Republicans were and where they lived. But one thing remained unchanged. Those Sundays that included church and fried-fish dinners nourished my soul, sustained my body, developed my mind, and increased my knowledge about politics, especially their impact on the lives of Indian people.

The combination of the Good News and good food has influenced many lives. I was no exception.

Love and War

Some people say that love is colorblind. But whoever said that didn't live in Robeson County in the 1950s. Love was a reality, yes. But colorblind love was most often forbidden by parents, discouraged by friends, dismissed by the community of all colors, and viewed as time wasted and an invitation for trouble. At least that's how I saw and experienced it then and on into the '60s.

This was no surprise, as white, Indian, and black people led separate lives in Robeson, and this was the engrained way of many generations. Some people didn't agree with this but knew that interracial dating was risky.

Yet, some Indian girls and women dated white boys and men, and some Indian boys and men dated white females. Usually, interracial dates took place in secret, or at least those involved took care not to let their families know. The biggest exception to this practice occurred at Pembroke State College, where, beginning in 1953, students were both Indian and white, as was the faculty and staff.

Some Indians believed that the reason white boys dated Indian girls was because of lust. That only increased some Indians' adamant stand against interracial dating; it also prompted some young Indian males to stalk and engage in verbal and physical attacks on any white males they believed might be of that mind-set.

From the time I began dating, I believed that some young men, both Indian and white, were gentlemen; similarly, some were "out for one thing," a phrase my Grandmother Smith used often. Dating someone who was black never crossed my mind. I'd never heard of anyone, white or Indian, doing so in Robeson County.

Though not many people favored interracial dating, the idea of marriage between Indian and white people was even more disturbing to many of the residents of the county. Aside from personal beliefs, religious doctrine, and social customs and practices, the legal aspect could not be ignored: *marriage between whites and nonwhites was prohibited by state law and had been since 1715.* A law also prohibited marriage between "Negroes and Cherokee Indians of Robeson County," the name given to the Lumbees at some point in the past. Anyone who defied this law could be sentenced to up to ten years in prison, and any minister or local official who officiated at such marriages could be charged with a misdemeanor crime and fined. Not many people would wage war not only against their families and friends but also against the county and state government. Love would be the loser.

Some interracial couples did marry, and they often involved a white man who married an Indian woman. In Saddletree, these white men (who were the fathers of several people I knew) were often soldiers who'd been stationed at one of the military bases in Fayetteville. Sometimes, an Indian woman married a white man who wasn't a soldier, but those men were usually from out of the county. I heard of instances of Indian men marrying white women; most often, they were not from Robeson County. These couples often lived elsewhere, though I knew of at least one faculty couple at Pembroke State College with an Indian husband and a white wife. I never knew of a white/Indian couple who were both natives of Robeson County marrying each other.

In any case, all the married interracial couples I knew who lived in Robeson County lived in Indian communities and adhered to the limitations placed on Indians in Robeson County. Two interracial couples were special friends of my parents. An Indian minister and his wife lived in Statesville, and one of my mother's childhood friends married a white man who was a career military officer stationed near Columbia, South Carolina. During their infrequent visits, my family warmly welcomed these couples to our home. How other interracial couples were treated was largely a matter of the attitudes and actions of their families and friends and the communities in which they lived.

Where did these mixed-race couples marry? How did they bypass the legal restriction against interracial marriage? Some were able to get a marriage license in North Carolina and other states because the Indian person could "pass for white" and did so. Some couples went to South Carolina, a short distance away, because the surnames of Indians were not as well-known there, and no one questioned them, especially if both the man and woman had medium to pale skin. The Marriage Chapel in Dillon, South Carolina, was a popular destination for Indians to marry and for Indians and whites to marry. That interracial marriage in South Carolina was illegal seemed of little concern. Some people said that cash, given as a tip, spoke louder than the law. I sometimes wondered if the phrase "All's fair in love and war" were really true.

I was told that some officials in certain North Carolina counties (and in parts of South Carolina) who didn't care about race or the law would issue a license to anyone. I was unaware of anyone who'd gotten married under those circumstances.

When I was in high school, the daughter of close family friends came home from out of state to be married to a white man who was also from out of state. It was a time of great joy for this family, and they planned a large, elaborate wedding.

The engaged couple went to the courthouse in Lumberton to get their marriage license. The bride-to-be, an attractive young woman, could have been white or Indian based on her appearance, but her surname was a very common Indian one. They were denied a marriage license because of the state's miscegenation law.

Apparently, someone in the marriage license office had spread the news about the young interracial couple applying for a license. Rumors quickly reached the bride's family that angry white people intended to harm the bridal party, disrupt the wedding, or both.

Friends of the bride's family were enraged. How dare someone threaten to harm this couple and their families because of their skin colors and love! A group of Indian men, with weapons I was told, stood watch over the family's home at night as the family prepared for the wedding. My uncle Henry Smith was one of the guardsmen.

Plans for the couple's wedding day changed. The young couple, their fathers, and the groom's brother dressed in street clothes and drove the short distance to Dillon, South Carolina. The bride cried as the miles sped by. This was not the way she had envisioned her wedding day.

After the marriage license was obtained, the groom's father, an ordained minister, married the beautiful, tear-stained young Indian woman to his handsome white son. The father of the bride and the brother of the groom served as witnesses. There was no joy at that brief ceremony, only torment and truth that the bride and her father fully understood.

The small group made their way back to Pembroke with a new bride whose face was wet from tears and heart was full of humiliation and pain. She was surrounded by men who loved her but were unable to stop her tears or provide comfort. The pain and embarrassment she felt were beyond the reach of words and hugs.

That night more than two hundred guests attended the wedding and said it was the loveliest one they'd ever attended. The beautiful bride and handsome groom reminded folks of Cinderella and her prince. Those who loved and knew the couple best wore small smiles and kept quiet about the ordeal of getting a marriage license, the marriage ceremony earlier in the day, and the possibility of mayhem and violence during the ceremony and afterward at the reception.

When I talked to my parents about this situation, they were appalled and angry. They spoke of the humiliation of the bride-to-be and her family and the confusion of the groom and his family. But their main focus was about the inhumaneness and ignorance of the situation. They spoke of God creating love and people. They emphasized the importance of love and marriage being able to occur without harassment, hate, and hurt. *Yes*, I thought. *That's the way it should be.* But obviously not everyone shared our thoughts about love and marriage.

A few years later, hate and harassment based on skin color and heritage came out in the open. The Grand Dragon of the South Carolina Ku Klux Klan, James "Catfish" Cole, declared war on the Lumbee Indians in Robeson and the surrounding counties. He was incensed because of what he called "race mixing" between whites and Indians in Robeson County. The specific incidents he mentioned were that a Lumbee family had moved into a predominantly white neighborhood in Lumberton, and a Lumbee woman in St. Pauls was reportedly dating a white man. Crosses were burned in both families' yards as warnings to those involved and to the Indian community at large. The Klan, "Catfish" Cole said, would not tolerate this kind of activity. He especially condemned any kind of romantic relationship between Indians and whites.

The grand dragon also took credit for burning a cross at a place where Indians gathered at night. "Catfish" Cole said the burning crosses were meant "to put Indians in their place, to end race mixing." He characterized Lumbees with malicious labels, including "mongrels" and "half-breeds." He passed the point of no return when he publicly stated that Indian women had "loose morals."

The grand dragon publicized a Klan gathering in a rented field outside of Maxton, just a few miles west of Pembroke. He emphasized that this rally would remind the Lumbees of "their place in the racial order." He spoke of the "mongrelization" of the races, referring to interracial interaction. The grand dragon called for five thousand Klan members to attend.

Indian people were angered by the burning crosses and what they meant, outraged by the slander and character assassination of Indian women, and aghast at the audacity of the grand dragon's appearance in a car with a loudspeaker publicizing the rally through downtown Pembroke. A group of Indian men, largely from the Pembroke area, devised a plan to humiliate and put the Klan and its leader in their place.

In the early-evening hours of January 18, 1958, in a field outside of Maxton, the grand dragon began his race-hating talk to a small group of supporters. A single lightbulb focused on him as he spoke. A gun fired abruptly, and the lightbulb shattered. "Catfish" Cole and his little band of fewer than one hundred small-minded followers were surprised by a group of Lumbee men intent on making it clear that racist and hate-filled talk about Lumbee people was not acceptable in Robeson County. With the shouts and whoops of Lumbee men ringing in their ears, the grand dragon and his followers ran and left the field as quickly as possible. Cameras snapped and reporters scribbled what they saw.

The grand dragon and his racist followers expected to receive support from the local white community and other communities across the state. Instead, Luther Hodges, the governor of North Carolina; Malcolm McLeod, the sheriff of Robeson County; and other elected officials denounced the Klan's motives and actions.

The "Battle of Hayes Pond" received not only statewide coverage but was also reported widely in national newspapers and magazines as well as on national television networks and shows. Most of the press condemned the Ku Klux Klan for its hate-inspired rhetoric and actions and portrayed the Klan's efforts at demeaning and controlling the Lumbees as ridiculous, laughable, and regrettable.

Leaders and individuals in many states, including North Carolina, commended the Lumbee leaders and men for their actions in protecting the honor and heritage of the Lumbee people. They agreed with the message they sent to "Catfish" Cole and his followers: Lumbee Indians are human beings who are proud of their heritage. The Klan will not terrorize Lumbee people; the Klan will not malign Lumbee women.

Lumbees and other American Indians in the state and across the nation rejoiced over the message delivered by Sanford Locklear, Neill

Lowery, Simeon Oxendine, and other Lumbee Indian men, including Uncle Henry Smith and Garth Locklear.

Instead of commendation, what "Catfish" Cole received was a criminal charge and conviction for inciting a riot. He was sentenced to two years in jail. The public war on romance and love between Indians and whites in Robeson County had ended.

But the Battle of Hayes Pond did not change the minds and hearts of many people about romance and love between Indians and whites. For many, the cross burnings and the routing of the Klan reemphasized the dangers of racial intermingling, especially those involving romance or love. Whether it was lust, romance, love, or marriage, most Indian people continued to share it with other Indians, just as they had before the Klan's crosses appeared on those dark winter nights.

I had no choices to make about the skin color of the young men I dated when I went to college. All the young men I met were white. As a freshman, I occasionally dated a basketball player at North Carolina State. During my sophomore year, he and a friend spent part of a weekend with our family. After the shock of seeing the height of these young men, my mom was her usual gracious self, though it was difficult for her to understand their fast-spoken accents. What caused her concern had nothing to do with their northern accents or skin color. When they asked, in her presence, what time Mass was conducted at the local Catholic church, her eyes reflected alarm. Like many southern people of the time, her knowledge of Catholicism was limited and often erroneous, but she kept her feelings to herself. My dad's reaction was to listen and maintain his trademark quiet politeness. The two basketball players and I went into Lumberton and found the Catholic church which they attended on Saturday evening. Mama seemed calmer when I stayed at home.

My Catholic friends from "up North" knew my heritage was American Indian and found that interesting but never asked questions about my life at home when we were in Raleigh or Robeson County. I didn't volunteer any information. If and when there was a need, I would explain tri-racial segregation.

But I admit that when it came to one young man, I did have some unspoken concerns that lasted through my college years. The bright, blond, and handsome landscape-architecture student I met and dated off and on while he was at NC State was friends with a young man from Lumberton. I wondered if the young man from Lumberton told the future landscape architect about the general taboo of whites and Indians having contact with each other, especially that of a romantic nature. But after a while, I disregarded those concerns and maintained contact with him, even after he left State and went to Harvard for graduate studies. His few visits to Robeson County evoked silent fears, for me, of both racist beliefs and behaviors. I was very aware that the war on romance and love among interracial couples still simmered in the heads and hearts of many. But young people of many heritages often disregarded barriers to romance. For a while, we were among them, whether he knew it or not.

When I was a junior in college, Carolyn Sampson, a beautiful Indian friend who was a student at Pembroke State, introduced me to a young white man from Red Springs. He, too, was a student at Pembroke, and we enjoyed each other's company on a regular basis when I went home for the weekend or visited with Carolyn at her home in Pembroke.

The young man's parents learned that their son was dating an Indian girl and gave him an ultimatum: quit dating the Indian girl or quit receiving any financial assistance for college or any other endeavor.

We were both stunned, as we had no idea that his parents knew of our dates. Realistically, neither of us should have been surprised. People of all races in Robeson watched what "their people" were doing. And many would happily make certain that this kind of news reached the ears of whomever would approve of it the least.

It didn't matter that my parents were college graduates with advanced degrees or that I was in college. Nor did it matter that my parents held no hatred or dislike for anyone because of their skin color or that their son was treated with respect in my home. The issue was racial heritage. In less than six months, the young man from Red Springs and I lost that battle in the war about love and race.

Romance and love were supposed to be fun and without fears, I thought. The reality was that I knew, and had known for many years, that skin color could and would affect relationships. But that didn't keep some of us from dreaming that, one day, we could love whomever we loved, wherever we were, without danger or darkness, without scorn or sarcasm, and without lying or lamenting about the law of the land we loved.

Love has always had a way of producing hope. And that hope kept many, including me, believing that love would find a way to be accepted and celebrated, no matter who was involved…even in Robeson County.

Tonsils, Teeth and Torture

*A*s a young child, my tonsils were frequently a source of pain. When home remedies didn't produce relief, a visit to a doctor was required. By the time I was in fifth grade, both doctors who treated me, Drs. Hooks and Pate in St.Pauls, recommended that my tonsils be removed. The sooner, the better, they said. Younger children recovered more quickly than older ones.

Those conversations produced immediate flashbacks of the tonsil clinic conducted at Magnolia School when I was not yet nine years old. How my school auditorium came to be a temporary medical facility is a mystery, but some older people in the community said that doctors and assistants came from the University of North Carolina School of Medicine in Chapel Hill and set up a mobile tonsillectomy unit. Others said it was organized by the Robeson County Health Department.

What I know with great certainty is that the large space that usually held chairs for school assemblies, programs, and basketball games became a giant hospital ward, complete with cots filled with quiet, sheet-covered children. Women in white uniforms moved from cot to cot and spoke softly to parents or other adults who were with the children on the cots. I never saw the operating area, but it was likely set up on the stage of the school auditorium. How and where the surgical instruments were sterilized also remains a mystery. The most pleasant sight I saw was some children eating ice cream.

When my dad discovered that I had walked into the mobile tonsil clinic, he spoke sternly to me: "You go home right now. You have no business being here."

Reluctantly, I followed his instruction. And I left without any ice cream.

Later that night, my parents talked about "the blessing of so many receiving medical care." What I wondered was if everyone got free ice cream. A few days later, that question was confirmed by classmates whose tonsils had been removed. They claimed that after they woke up after having their tonsils removed, they ate as much Buttercup ice cream as they wanted. But I very much doubted that. There were too many children in that auditorium/hospital room to give that much ice cream for free. They probably dreamed it.

It wasn't until I was in the sixth grade that the decision was made to have my tonsils removed. But my experience would be very different from the one I'd witnessed briefly at school. My tonsils would be removed at Highsmith Hospital in Fayetteville. According to my parents, Dr. Robinson, the physician who cared for my dad's eyes, would remove the troublesome tonsils, and I would spend at least one night in the hospital. No, it wouldn't hurt while the doctor was performing the procedure, my parents assured me. And yes, I would get ice cream to eat afterward. All that I wanted, and my choice of flavors, too!

Unafraid, I, in pajamas, rode with my parents to Fayetteville. We found our way to the hospital on Hay Street, the main street of this big town, and very soon I was sitting in a chair that looked very similar to one you might find in a dentist's office. The nurse was pleasant and gently placed a helmetlike contraption on my head. Her instructions were to just get comfortable, breathe naturally, and count backward from ten to one.

The next thing I knew, I was in a strange bed, and I heard loud noises in the room. Sounds of car horns blowing, brakes squealing, people talking, and was that a train whistle blowing? How could one relax with all that going on? And no, I didn't want any ice cream. My throat felt strange. It was hard to swallow. Actually, my throat hurt. Maybe some ice cream would help. Again, no, I didn't want ice cream of any flavor or any amount.

Could I please just go home? Not today, I was told. So there I was, stuck in a hospital bed with a very sore throat and a nurse asking and then pleading with me to eat ice cream or drink a tiny bit of Pepsi-Cola, while I had no desire for anything to drink or eat.

And sleep? Impossible! The noises scared me, and my mind seemed to be playing tricks on me. Or was I dreaming? Those wild animals that I saw while sitting in that weird chair—where did they come from? And where did they go? Would they return if I went to sleep? I certainly wouldn't ask my mother, who was spending the night with me. She might call one of the nurses, and who knew what they'd suggest. It would probably be something about ice cream.

I did eat ice cream eventually, and I sipped lukewarm Pepsi and finally got to go home. But it didn't happen the day after the tonsillectomy or even the day after that. My parents spoke quietly about how fortunate it was that my tonsil removal had been done at a hospital. They mentioned complications, and I heard them say something about me bleeding more than expected. But the only complicated thing to me was the mystery of the wild animals. Whenever I returned to school again, I'd certainly ask my classmates who'd had their tonsils removed at school about the wild animals.

Some of my classmates said that that they'd also heard strange things during their tonsil-removal experience. But they didn't remember any wild animals in Technicolor. Another unsolved mystery that I just wanted to forget.

⌒

Long before the tonsil experience, my reaction to the announcement that I had a dental appointment was drastically different from having my tonsils removed. I was afraid! My fear was that the dentist would pull out all my teeth. This stemmed from conversations I'd heard from young classmates about people who had not one tooth left in their heads after going to the dentist.

My first experience going to "old Dr. Moore" in St. Pauls created apprehension, but Dr. Moore was kind and occasionally even smiled. Most important, I felt no pain and left with all my teeth. The second visit consisted of drilling and filling. Both the sounds and the procedures hurt. It took exactly two visits for the word "dentist" to become synonymous with dread, fear, and pain.

The dread, fear, and pain intensified when my mother began to take me to the son of old Dr. Moore in Lumberton. "Young Dr. Moore" was a stern-looking man who never spoke other than to his assistant, whose attention seemed to focus on her recently painted fingernails. He offered no words of support or comfort as he jabbed a needle into my gums. His technique of administering a shot was harsh and always caused pain and silent tears. And if any painkiller was in the needle, then it was overshadowed by the pain caused by the injection. Young Dr. Moore never inquired if more anesthetic were needed or perhaps a short break might be beneficial. Visits to the dentist were utter torture.

My mother insisted that each visit to young Dr. Moore's office would be less painful, less traumatic. But that wasn't true for me. And another thing didn't change, either. All the patients my brothers and I saw were white people. After a few years, we concluded that we got treated because our parents had enough money to pay for the work, but we were not really welcome. Surely, he was kinder and caused less pain to white people like himself. We believed that the torture was the payment for being Indians.

Yes, there were times when I faked illness to postpone the agony of having dental work done. That continued throughout high school and college. This brown girl would not voluntarily make or keep an appointment for torture. My mother made certain that I did.

hile my parents were financially able to provide professional medical care for my brothers and me, few physicians welcomed Indians. Two who did were located in St. Pauls and shared an office building; Drs. Hooks and Pate provided medical care for my brothers and me when we were very young. On call day and night, they were courteous and kind. We sat in the waiting room with white and other Indian people. It was a great relief that I didn't have to worry that a staff member would make hurtful comments about my skin color, as had happened years before in Lumberton. At the time, I believed the people of St. Pauls were friendlier to Indians than those in Lumberton. But I couldn't prove it was true for others.

Later, our family's physician was Dr. Frank McGrath in Lumberton. Fortunately, I didn't need to visit him often, but when I did, he was always respectful, professional, and competent. That's all I'd ever wanted from anyone, so I was grateful he was available when needed. That my parents continued to be patients of Dr. McGrath reinforced my belief that he was respectful of them as well.

It was very obvious during my childhood that medical care for Indians in Robeson County, including basic care for common ailments, was severely lacking. The reality was that many Indian people simply couldn't afford any kind of professional medical attention. But even sadder and more chilling was the attitude of most medical professionals in Robeson County. Despite their allegiance to the Hippocratic oath, most physicians adhered to the highly engrained social custom of the community, which was that white, black, and Indian people did not intermingle. Most medical professionals were unwilling to risk the furor, likely ostracism, and financial loss that would have resulted. That meant that very few white physicians were willing to treat Indians.

Even when Indians did receive medical attention, many adults were of the opinion that it was inferior to what white patients received. Such was the case with a member of our extended family. One of my dad's uncles, Rufus Martin, lived in Pembroke and was a well-respected carpenter. He became extremely ill and was taken to a hospital in Lumberton that had separate wards for white, black, and Indian people.

The family was told that all the rooms for Indians were occupied, so my dad's uncle was given a bed and placed in the hall. It soon became apparent to his family that the medical staff was not checking on him or providing any care.

Alarmed and afraid, Lindy Martin, the ill man's son, called my dad and asked if he could somehow intervene. None of us ever learned who my dad contacted, but my dad's uncle was moved to a room, received medical care, and survived the harrowing experience. His family always believed that the poor attention and lack of treatment he received was a result of racial identity and racism.

At that time, there were no American Indian doctors in Robeson County. In fact, American Indians were not allowed to attend medical or dental schools in North Carolina. Those Indians who chose medical professions as careers were forced to attend school out of state. Some became military doctors, and others practiced out of state. It was 1958 when Dr. Martin Brooks, a Lumbee Indian and honors graduate of the University of Michigan medical school, opened a general medical practice in Pembroke and had the first integrated waiting room in Robeson County. He encountered racism and resistance in gaining hospital privileges for his patients at the hospital in Lumberton.

The infrequent free dental and tonsillectomy clinics for Magnolia School students may have caused some brief pain or torture, but ultimately, they were the source of freedom from pain. Far too many people, including children, never visited a doctor or dentist and suffered far too much because they were poor Indians. That Indians died because of lack of medical attention was a shameful and sad part of life that seemed unimportant to many of those who could have prevented it.

The pain that hurt me the most in my growing-up years was never diagnosed by the local medical profession. Unfortunately, no medicine on drugstore counters or remedies concocted by people in the community would cure or diminish the pain. The torture of racism continued for Indian people even as I, a child, hoped a cure would be found soon.

Mulberry Memories

*J*ames Walter Smith and Lela Locklear Smith were my mother's parents. In many ways, they were opposites. He was several years older than his bride, who was less than eighteen years old when they married. Granddaddy was tall and broad shouldered and seemed to listen carefully before responding. Or that was my impression. Grandmother was short and round and asked pointed, direct questions. She expressed her opinions freely and strongly, whether asked or not.

My Smith grandparents had five children who survived, and my mother was the oldest. Two of their children, Aunt Shirley and Uncle Henry, and their families lived nearby. Uncle Joe and his family lived with our grandparents until they moved to Cary, North Carolina, when I was in elementary school. After her marriage, Aunt Vickie and her family lived in suburban Washington, DC. Uncle Millard and his family's home was in suburban Boston.

According to others, Granddaddy Smith was a barber, teacher, and the first Indian postmaster in Pembroke. What I remember is that he was a Methodist minister who served small Indian churches in southeastern North Carolina and near Dillon, South Carolina, during my childhood and till his death in 1955. He received no regular salary but was instead paid from offerings collected on the Sundays when he preached; this provided limited economic stability for his family. During my child-hood, Grandmother was acutely aware of this situation and sometimes commented about it: "You know the amount of that Sunday offering didn't pay for the gas to get to that church and back home. And how about when there's a funeral or a Bible study? Preachers' families have to eat and pay bills, too."

Though she lamented the difficulty of much work and little pay for Granddaddy, he continued to pray and preach. His peers and the people he served highly praised his work and service as a Methodist minister.

Granddaddy was said to have taught Grandmother how to read and write. We were told she became a leading voice in the Pembroke community for the education of Indian children and adults and also supported equality and empowerment for women. Her participation in church activities was widely recognized. But Grandmother Smith's main focus was always her family; for years, this meant keeping Walter and her children fed and in clean and ironed clothes, teaching the children good manners, encouraging them to get as much education as possible, and reminding the girls to "keep your skirts down." Later, she stressed behaving well and acquiring a good education to her grandchildren. And, for her granddaughters, her additional advice was to "keep your legs crossed."

It was only about twenty miles to Pembroke, where my mother's parents lived. But as a young child, their way of life seemed as if it might have been from another country. Within walking distance from my grandparents' home to the heart of the "no-stoplight town" was a drugstore, movie theater, beauty and barber shop, gas station, café, and even a jewelry store. Indians owned many of the businesses, and Indian people were welcomed as customers. Pates Supply Company, the largest business in Pembroke, offered clothes, shoes, groceries, and hardware items for cash or payment at the end of the month (if one's credit record were suitably sound, according to the white owner). The Locklear Funeral Home, owned by Mr. Luther Locklear, a relative of my grandmother's, was available when needed. It horrified me when I learned that Mr. Luther and his family lived on the second floor of the funeral home. No way would I agree to live where dead people were lying in caskets open for viewing just a few steps away—especially at bedtime. How could anyone sleep?

Closer to my grandparents' home was the First Methodist Church, where several members of my mother's family were members. It was where my mother's youngest sister, Vickie, married David Ransom in a beautiful night wedding with candles burning brightly. Not yet six years old at the time, I was one of the two excited and happy flower girls—until I tripped on the altar steps following what I thought was a fairy-tale event.

Attending worship services at First Methodist was an eye-opening experience. Physical exercise was part of the service. Sit and stand; sit and stand! But there was even more to cause amazement; prayers were read in unison out of a book instead of individuals making spontaneous pleas and promises. I wondered if the exercises and prayer readings were just unusual ways of getting us to pay attention.

By the time I was in the seventh or eighth grade, I was accustomed to the order of worship but was puzzled by something much more important. The entire congregation proclaimed that they believed in the "holy catholic church." That statement raised serious theological questions for me and went unanswered for more years than I care to admit. My childhood religious instruction and understanding was spelled in seven letters: B-A-P-T-I-S-T. Back then, Baptist and Catholic were as far apart, in my mind, as South and North.

Our visits to our Smith grandparents often took place on Sunday afternoons, once or twice a month. Sometimes others were present, including Uncle Henry and his family (who lived almost in our grandparents' backyard) and Aunt Shirley, who lived nearby. The adults always talked with one another, and sometimes the conversations grew intense when local schools or politics was the topic. I learned by middle-school age that my parents and her siblings often differed in their views. Daddy was sometimes noticeably quieter during those discussions. When we were older, my brothers and I decided that Daddy's Sunday visits to Pembroke decreased because he didn't want to be part of discussions that held no place for differing opinions or amicable endings.

When the voices of her visiting grandchildren grew too loud or their actions became rambunctious, no matter what season it was, Grandmother Smith directed the young ones to "go play in the back-yard under the mulberry tree." She believed that the best place for children to be was where playing and horsing around took place far enough to protect her home and furnishings but close enough to keep the kids in line. All of us young ones knew that misbehavior, as judged by Grandmother Lela, would not go unnoticed. Either our parents or she herself would set us straight.

Each year in mid- to late summer, Uncle Millard and his family came to Robeson County to visit, as did Aunt Vickie and her family. It was if they were visiting royalty. My mother and other members of the family invited each out-of-state family for a meal. All the delicious food, fine china, beautiful table linens, lively conversations, and hearty laughter were enough to make those occasions memorable. But it was the strange accents of the Boston relatives and one young male cousin's insistence on patting my hair that entertained me the most.

At least once during the summer visits of our northern relatives, we all gathered at our grandparents' home. And it was during that time together that all the cousins invariably found ourselves in the backyard under the broad branches of the mulberry tree. Cousins of all ages played, fought, talked, lied, cried, told secrets, and shared dreams so farfetched they could only be spoken in whispers. But we also under-stood or learned quickly that the mulberry tree could be the source and site of punishment for anyone whose behavior was less than desir-able. Under the mulberry tree, country and city cousins from South and

North became one family—the Walter and Lela Smith family—at least for that afternoon and part of the night.

But the mulberry tree was not just a space for children. Under the mulberry tree, peas were shelled, corn was shucked, lye soap was made, and clothes were boiled in a large black cast-iron pot till they met the Lela Smith stamp of "sanitary." The branches of the mulberry tree provided privacy and protection from the blazing sun for the adult children of Walter and Lela Smith as they shared their dreams, fears, and hopes with their parents.

Other memories from visits to my Smith grandparents' home that have lasted include my fascination with a china cabinet full of salt and pepper shakers. No one was allowed to touch or use them, but the urge to do so was great. Grandmother collected those treasures on trips she and Granddaddy made to visit their children, relatives, and friends.

And the organ! It was an old pump organ with wood stained the color of ripened black walnuts. The keys were usually hidden under the sliding wooden cover that was part of the tall musical wonder, and children were forbidden to play on or around it. My mother played it growing up, and after several years of piano instruction, I was finally given permission to play "What a Friend We Have in Jesus" on that treasured possession of Grandmother Lela's. It was a "grown-up" moment for me. I never admitted that my legs and feet were near exhaustion from the effort of pumping while playing that old hymn.

My favorite activity involving my Smith grandparents was spending time with my cousin Pat at our grandparents' home. My birthday was four months earlier than hers, and we both had brothers. Though our activities were nothing unusual for children of early elementary school age, our bond was strong. Our time together was special to me.

One memory that involved our brothers became a Smith family legend. Pat's brother Mike and my brothers were playing under the mulberry tree when Cousin Loretta Smith decided to take or play with something that my brother Franklin had. Pleading for its return had no effect on Loretta. Mike, Pat's younger brother, and Cam threatened to throw Loretta into the well that was situated at the side of our grand-parents' home. And yes, the well had some water in it.

Yelling and screaming soon brought Grandmother Lela out-side to find out what the situation was. When she learned the details, Grandmother ordered Cam and Mike to march straight into the smoke-house, a small, dark shed that held unknown objects and the possibility of living creatures that preferred darkness. The only light in the smoke-house was a tiny line of light one could see through a keyhole. Only after the return of Mama and Aunt Lula, the mothers of the bad-boy brigade, did Cam and Mike return to daylight and civilization. How long that was depends on who is asked, but it was long enough to make a life-lasting impression on the two banished boy cousins and all who saw or heard about the Well Episode.

Grandparents who lived in town, aunts, uncles, and cousins both near and far away, feasts, fun, and fights were all part of the visits with my Smith grandparents. Some would say there's nothing extra special about those experiences. And they may be right. But they are mine, and mulberry memories last.

The Difference

Many people in Robeson County thought my dad was a native Robesonian, but he was always quick to correct them, as did I. As a native of Person County, he was extremely proud of his heritage and relatives who were members of the people known as the High Plains or Person County Indians. When I was a young child, the total number of the group was approximately five hundred, including those who lived away from the High Plains community.

The central part of the High Plains community, ten to twelve miles north of Roxboro in Person County, could be reached by traveling several miles on either highway 501 headed to South Boston or 49 in the direction of Virgilina. Both towns were located in Virginia. Leaving state highways, the remainder of the trip was on dirt roads. Most of the Indian people connected to the community by blood, marriage, and tradition lived near the boundaries of both North Carolina and Virginia. My dad's parents lived in North Carolina and received mail at the Christie, Virginia, post office, a few miles from their home.

The High Plains community had red clay soil, rolling hills, unpaved roads, and no electricity nor telephones, and toilets were outside when I was young. Or at least that was true at the home of my grandparents,

Alexander (known as Zan) and Mary Martin Epps, and the homes of my immediate relatives. Drinking water was dipped from a natural spring located across the dirt road in front of my grandparents' home. A slight hill midway across the path on the far side of the road made carrying two buckets of water back to the house a task for adults and strong, nimble young people.

The "home-house," as my grandparents' home was called, was a simple two-story wooden structure with a porch that covered the width of the house. The porch was often the center of lively conversations, especially on warm Sunday afternoons when family and friends came to visit. It was also a place from which adults could keep a quiet eye on the "chaps," the name for children who were not yet young adults and needed a watchful eye on their activities. Until I was discovered and sent to the yard to play, it was from one of the windows on that porch where I listened and watched as my aunt Lois Epps Jones labored to give birth to her son Larry.

There were two front doors with a single window next to each door. The door on the right side of the porch opened to the room that doubled as a sitting room and bedroom for my grandparents. A fireplace provided heat in the winter and some light. Occasionally, the fireplace was the target of Granddaddy's chewing tobacco juice.

The other door led to the front room (I called it the company room), which contained a sofa, double bed, and a wood-burning heater that was rarely used unless my grandparents had extra guests or upon a special occasion such as Christmas. At Christmastime, the front room held a cedar tree, cut from the woods on the land, adorned with home-made decorations. When I was a preteen, a dark-stained upright piano became a permanent fixture in the room. It was a special treat when Cousin Joel Stewart played it and the adults hummed or sang gospel hymns. Later, Cousin Dorothy Stewart carried on that tradition.

The kitchen was located at the back of the house and contained a wood-burning cookstove, which made it the warmest room in the house in the winter. It was the best-smelling room year round; the aromas of

Grandmother's cooking filled the air and tantalized the tummies of all who were nearby. Mealtime found Granddaddy Zan sitting at the head of the large rectangular wooden table. With no advance warning, he bowed his head and murmured his brief blessing of the food: "Thank God for breakfast" or whatever other meal had been prepared.

Upstairs were two bedrooms that were reached by climbing extremely steep stair steps. The first bedroom was a large open space with two very small windows, two double beds and a closet that contained both clothes and shelves with canned foods. This was the room that my brothers and I shared when we visited. Grandmother's quilts were made into pallets and used for additional young visitors.

The second bedroom was smaller and had one double bed. This room also had a window, and because of the size of the window, the room had much more light in it than the other upstairs bedroom. When Dad's youngest brother, Caleb (better known as Whit), married, he and his bride occupied the smaller bedroom for a while.

Wintertime heat for the upstairs bedrooms was provided by layers of quilts. We learned quickly that any "necessary" visits should be made before being weighted down with the heaviness and warmth of those quilts made of scrap pieces of materials and stitched together with love by Grandmother Mary and other female family members. Summertime, it was hot upstairs as the windows were rarely opened. This was especially so when two or more children slept in one double bed.

Furnishings throughout the home were sparse and simple. The focal point of the sitting room was a mantel clock above the fireplace that loudly donged the hours. At night, oil lamps cast soft shadows in the room where the family gathered.

Making money to support a family was difficult for High Plains Indians. Most were farmers, because that's how generations before them had earned a living. Only a few men made a living doing other kinds of work: there were few places nearby to work, and discrimination against Indians was both legal and widely practiced. Surprisingly, in all my years of visiting, from early childhood through college, I heard few complaints. And those were more concerns about how the weather might affect the crops than any specific laments about the long hours of physical labor, the meager income, or even the amount of time spent driving to the rare job located many miles away.

Economic hardships did not affect these families as one might expect. No time was spent discussing the lack of money or material things—at least not in the presence of children. The women made many of the clothes for themselves and their children. Clothes and shoes were handed down to the next child, if they were still wearable. Quilts were made from scraps of leftover material and clothes that could no longer be worn. And, except for sugar, coffee, flour, and a few other staples, most of the food was grown or raised at home. Shelves were filled with canned goods in the summer, and hams were hung in the smokehouse behind the kitchen in the fall for the snowy days and cold nights of winter.

The elders among my High Plains relatives never focused on earthly income or possessions. They had their sights on eternal rewards. Even in the rare correspondence that we had with our High Plains relatives, a reference always included love and hope for the future. My aunt Viola always signed her letters and Christmas cards with the closing words "Love and prayers."

Our family always visited my Epps grandparents at least once during the summer months and shortly after Christmas. A winter visit almost always included snow-covered ground. For children from the flatlands, where snow was a rarity, the all-white, gently rolling hills and frozen, deeply rutted dirt roads leading to the home-house produced both excitement and fright. Sitting in a cold car unable to go any farther created anxiousness. Having horses pull the car out of the frozen ruts, with Mama, Brother, Cam, and me inside, was exciting, especially after it was over. My grandmother always smiled as my dad unpacked a bagful of oranges, and my granddaddy always mumbled his thanks when he received Black Moriah chewing tobacco. He nodded his head in gratitude to my mother for bringing past issues of *Look* and *Life* magazines.

Even though he could neither read nor write, he spent hours looking at the photographs in those publications. I often wondered what he thought, but children didn't ask reasons of adults in High Plains. It was just what he did.

Relatives and friends were constantly coming and going during the Christmas season, but mostly the house was full of aunts, uncles, and cousins. It was a special treat if my dad's brother Alfred was there, as he always lived far away (including Europe) because of his military career. If the family wasn't talking, then we were eating. And always, we had plenty of good things from which to choose. Canned cherries, which my aunts and uncles claimed my grandparents only served when my dad visited, were my favorite, as were the coconut pies.

Summer visits brought walks with aunts and cousins to get drinking and cooking water from the spring, time with Grandmother Mary in the big vegetable garden encircled with flowers, hours spent listening to adult relatives talk about whatever was of interest to them, and (infrequently) riding with an adult to the Christie general store to get mail and maybe a piece of candy. It was always fun spending time with my cousins. A variety of ages, both younger and older, we "chaps" talked, laughed, conducted pretend church, and stayed out of the way of adults, as we knew we should.

But by far, the best times were those I spent with my cousin Nancy Martin, a daughter of Aunt Elizabeth (the oldest of my dad's sisters) and her husband, Uncle John Martin. Nancy was the sister I always wanted but didn't have. With only three months difference in our ages, we bonded early and deeply. Though our time with each other was brief on most winter and summer visits, we made many special memories.

One summer when I was eight or nine years old, my parents allowed me to stay with my grandparents an extra week after my parents had returned to our home. Because everyone knew how much my cousin Nancy and I enjoyed each other's company, we spent much time together. We spent hours outdoors while the adults "cropped" tobacco and Grandmother cooked dinner for the crowd of relatives who helped

Granddaddy Zan harvest tobacco. We were together on days when we had nothing planned as well, just playing or hanging around. All the adults and older cousins said we were spoiled. We never disputed those comments. We just kept on enjoying each other's company.

A very special event also occurred that summer. I was allowed to rise early one Sunday morning and ride to South Boston with Aunt Docia Ree and Aunt Lois and whoever drove them there. They were members of a group of High Plains people who sang gospel songs before Uncle Willie Lee Stewart, who was married to another of my dad's sisters, Aunt Gladys, preached during a live radio broadcast. Of course, we returned to High Plains in time to attend church. And there were no complaints about hearing two sermons on one Sunday!

It was a bit different one summer when both my brothers and I spent a week or two with our Epps grandparents. I was expected to help mind the boys, and they were full of energy and ideas for entertainment that often didn't match with what Grandmother Mary or I considered appropriate. One time, my brothers and I had visited Uncle John and Aunt Elizabeth's family nearby and were walking home. They picked vegetables and flowers from a garden without permission. When Grandmother discovered this, she scolded the boys for stealing, walked them back to Uncle John's, and made them confess their wayward activity. On the return walk, she "switched" the little boys' legs as punishment for their wrongdoing. It was the only time I ever saw Grandmother be upset or punish a child. It was also the only time my little brothers took anything from a garden in High Plains without permission.

During that summer visit with my brothers, they had many playmates. Uncle Petey and Aunt Louise had a large family, and all but two children were boys. Those cousins and the sons of Aunt Sally and Uncle Clarence Epps were frequent visitors. It never ceased to amaze me that even with their rambunctious play and mischievous antics, my brothers and their cousins were not chastised with raised voices by any adult. Quiet, firm voices made it clear how to behave, and my young brothers and cousins understood and followed those instructions.

While family gatherings were the primary social functions in High Plains, one special event was the Indian community's celebration of the Fourth of July at the High Plains Indian School. I looked forward to the lemonade prepared in and served from metal tubs.

The High Plains Indian School was initially constructed on land donated by Green Martin and later by Ditrion Epps, relatives of both my grandparents. A unique feature of the school was that financial support came from both North Carolina and Virginia. The High Plains Indian School was a source of community pride and hope. No matter what grade the children were in, academics and disciplined behavior were stressed and expected of them. Parents understood and supported the value of education. They were allies of the principal and teachers, who were usually white, and they encouraged their children to learn, not loaf.

During my early childhood, formal classroom education for the High Plains Indians ended at grade seven, just as it had when my dad was a student. The first high school graduation was held in 1952, and there were five graduates, including two of my first cousins, Stella Martin and Emma Epps. Stella continued her education in nursing school, and Emma entered Campbell College. Both were widely praised for their accomplishments.

But as important as the school was to my dad's home community, the heart of the High Plains community was the church. The church that I remember well was Calvary Baptist Church, located about one mile from the school. The small brick structure with a simple steeple had lovely wooden pews and stained-glass windows all of the same pattern. High Plains Indians gathered faithfully on Sundays for instruction about the Bible during Sunday school.

While singing was an important part of the worship service at Calvary Baptist, it was the preaching of God's Word that was of the highest priority. Adults listened attentively and reverently. Children of all ages heard the Word, too, whether it was of interest or not. Salvation, hope, and heaven were the themes I recall. But what I remember most vividly was that all the pastors when I was young were white men with some level of seminary training. They made their points, sometimes in soft, conversational tones and at other times in louder voices. But I never feared that the preacher would have a stroke, and no "scorpions" skittered across the walls behind the pulpit. Both were differences from my home church that I considered positive.

After church, Grandmother Epps, along with one or more of her daughters or daughters-in-law, completed the preparations for a large dinner that usually included one or more aunts, uncles, and their many children. In the summertime, most of the food came fresh from the garden. In the winter, the vegetables came from the many glass jars of canned vegetables and fruits lined neatly on shelves in an upper bedroom. Little meat was served, but always there was dessert, usually a number of different kinds of pies. It always amazed me that though Grandmother was diabetic and followed a very strict diet, she cooked the pies without recipes. And I never saw her sneak a bite at any time. No matter what season of the year, Sunday dinners were a time to give thanks, relax, and enjoy the company of family members.

By the time I was in college, I realized that there was something very different about my High Plains relatives. Even with poverty surrounding many of them or being a constant threat, a blanket of quiet peace seemed to enfold them much of the time. When tragedy or sorrow struck, the family mourned together and moved on slowly into the future. When a family member's actions or words created a disappointment or betrayed family values, it was acknowledged, and the person responsible for the dismay was usually given words of counsel as well as support and loyalty. Blessings that came created joy- filled hearts for everyone. Faith and fortitude were daily family companions.

Years later, I finally learned what made my High Plains family so different. Aunt Lois told me that the lives of the Zan and Mary Epps family were based on love. Always first, there was love of God. And that was followed quickly and closely by love of family. In good or bad times, unconditional love undergirded every family member, every relationship, every day of every year.

Was this true for all Indian families in the High Plains community? I simply don't know. But I am certain that unconditional love made a big difference in the lives of the Zan and Mary Epps family. Just ask anyone with that connection—and that includes me.

Community Life-Photographs

Congregation of Ten Mile Center Baptist Church, Highway 301 north of Lumberton

Mama's parents, Lela Locklear Smith and James Walter Smith

Daddy's parents, Mary Martin Epps and Zan Epps

High Plains Indian School

Calvary Baptist Church, High Plains Road, north of Roxboro

Magnolia School Years

The Four Rs

Long before I was old enough to do so, I wanted to go to school. That my family lived in a house at the edge of the grounds of Magnolia School where both my parents worked was reason enough. But from a very early age, I was interested in words and books. I wanted to go to school to read more than the random words I'd learned from purchased goods: corn, coffee, bread, milk, and newspapers.

When at last I entered Magnolia School in 1947, a month or so before I was six years old, grades one through twelve were all housed in one attractive brick one-story building. Each classroom had plenty of light flowing in from windows that were high enough that young children couldn't see outside. The main entrance was midway within the building, and the school had two smaller entrances on the north and south ends. The principal's office was located at the south end of the hall, not far away from the first-grade classroom. School buses parked on the north end of the school property and were clearly visible from our home.

Miss Mary (Mrs. Mary Hammonds Locklear, from Saddletree and Pembroke) was the much-beloved first-grade teacher. Short, with dark curls and eyes that sparkled, she was patient and professional, kind and ready to reassure us or wipe away our tears, and she just loved to teach "her children" how to read. Though easygoing and fun, she corrected and guided us gently in how to share and interact with one another. I loved Miss Mary from the first day and have happy memories of learning how to read, trying to draw, and, with my classmates, singing the many songs she taught us.

Grades two and three were real work, and both Miss Betty Lou Bell and Miss Gertrude Locklear expected full attention and near-perfect behavior. It was in each of these classrooms where I became aware that the school did not have enough books on every subject for each student. Often, the students who didn't have a full set of books didn't attend every day; when they were present, they shared books with whomever sat nearby. I wondered how they would complete their homework, but I assumed the teacher had a plan that worked.

The third grade brought much excitement because we now had a music teacher. I knew about this before school started, since my dad, the principal of Magnolia School, had interviewed the prospective teacher, and my mother had prepared a fine meal for the visitor from "up North." Mr. Charles Katzenjammer came from the state of New York and talked very fast and had very pale skin. But he was nice and offered to teach me piano, so I soon forgot about the sound and pace of his speech.

It was a special year when I entered the fourth grade. A new school building was used for grades four through twelve, while the primary grades and the auditorium that doubled as an assembly space and gymnasium remained in the old school building. The old and new buildings were connected by a wide, covered walkway. On rainy days, between the change of classes and during lunch hour, some of the male high school teachers and students used it as a place to smoke cigarettes.

For many adults and students, the long, low, flat-roofed, contemporary design of the new building was an architectural oddity. A long hallway with lockers and tile floors contained both the elementary and high school classrooms, including a science classroom with sinks and areas for the dissection of animals and for learning about chemical compounds. Off a shorter hallway near the entrance to the building was the library, a home-economics classroom, and a large cafeteria. Away from the back of the new building was the favorite place of many students, a huge playing field.

The teachers were delighted with their new lounge, which had a private restroom for them and a couple of sofas and chairs where they could enjoy adult conversations without students around. On rare occasions when the door of the teachers' lounge was open for more than a few seconds, a thin haze of smoke was clearly visible. We thought nothing of teachers smoking cigarettes in those days.

With the completion of the new school building, the enrollment of the Magnolia School greatly increased once "feeder schools" in the northern end of the county sent additional Indian students. Now, instead of one class of each grade, the school had two classrooms for grades one through eight.

Who my fourth-grade teacher would be created a dilemma for me. I thought both Miss Hazel Locklear and Miss Gladys Locklear were two of the most pleasant and beautiful women I'd ever met. Though their personalities differed dramatically—Miss Hazel was quiet and elegant, while Miss Gladys was bubbly and pretty—I wanted both for my teacher. I asked my dad if I could spend half the year in each of their classes. He responded with a half-smile and a quiet no.

The bubbly Miss Gladys was my teacher, though I did spend some time with Miss Hazel in the afternoons performing any tasks she would allow me to do or just visiting for a few minutes with her. Young and vivacious, Miss Gladys had few disciplinary problems in the class because many of the boys were in love with her, and many of the girls were taken with her looks and manner.

My real delight in fourth grade was reading, and the high point of any day was going to the library, where Miss Mary Deese, the librarian, greeted us with a smile. Many things interested me, but what I enjoyed most were biographies. Men, women, living or dead—it didn't matter.

I often found a book or two and sat on the floor, lost in the life of another in different places, times, and circumstances.

The fourth grade was also the year when Magnolia School hired its first art teacher, Mr. Stanton Lockley. A year or two later, when Mr. Lockley left to join the air force and become a pilot, Miss Margaret Martin from Maryland joined the faculty. A white, middle-aged woman with unruly salt-and-pepper hair, Miss Martin instructed us in painting (both representational and contemporary styles) as well as pottery making and sculpture. Not content to have us create for ourselves and our families, she entered the work of several students in state contests. Many of us were stunned to learn that our work had been awarded prizes or honorable mentions. Gloria Morrison (and now Lowery) was among her gifted students; she later studied art in college and became a well-known and much-respected Lumbee artist.

Grades five through eight brought an array of teachers with different personalities and teaching styles. All were sincere and consistent in their efforts to instruct and discipline us well. One example of the personality and dedication of my teachers was Mr. Woodrow Sampson, my sixth-grade teacher. He was known as a very strict disciplinarian who absolutely did not tolerate sassiness, out-of-turn talking, late homework, or undue rowdiness in the classroom, on the playground, in the cafeteria, or while walking in the halls. Punishment was swift and often included the use of a paddle.

The dedication and creativity of his teaching included a unit on the solar system. Along with the usual textbook study, our class made scale-size replicas of the planets; we then painted them and hung them in the classroom. We learned facts and spelling and English as we learned about Jupiter and Mars, and we invited other classes and their teachers to see our work. This project remains in my mind as not only the highlight of that sixth-grade year but of grades seven and eight as well.

Another memorable educational lesson and event took place away from the classroom. Mr. Sampson received permission to take the entire class to his home in the heart of the Saddletree community, several miles away, to watch the coronation of Queen Elizabeth. Though the television screen appeared to be covered with giant snowflakes much of the time, we sat on chairs, sofas, and the floor and heard the entire ceremony and caught glimpses of the young queen's elaborate coronation ceremony. As a delicious bonus (and at his expense), Mr. Sampson prepared a picnic for us, complete with hot dogs and ice cream.

Miss Ophelia Thomas, Miss Artie Emanuel, and Mr. Adolph Dial were my teachers for fifth, seventh, and eighth grades, respectively, and they, too, expended considerable effort in developing our minds and manners. The dedication of all who were my teachers, as well as of Miss Bonnie Lowry (who amazed all of us with her beautiful left-handed penmanship), Mr. George Emanuel, Mr. Robert McGirt, and Mr. Barto Clark Jr.—all of whom were also teachers of grades five through eight—was a gift, whether my classmates and I realized it or not.

Completing the eighth grade was a major milestone for many Magnolia students, as their parents had not achieved that educational level. Often, it wasn't the reading, 'riting, or 'rithmetic that created the failure: it was rampant racism that affected all the Indian schools in Robeson County.

⟨～⟩

*E*ntering high school was exciting for me, but probably less so than for many of the students at other high schools. Magnolia High School students had classrooms and shared the library, cafeteria, and restrooms in the same building, as did grades four through eight. Our day started and ended at the same time as other students, since all students rode the same buses to school. By eighth grade, we all knew the high school teachers, if not personally then at least by sight and name.

What was different in high school was the changing of classes for different subjects and having a study hall. Whether we went to Mr. Johnny Blanks'class for endless pages of diagramming sentences in English or listening to his precise teaching of this country's history, to math classes taught by the brilliant and nattily dressed Mr. Herbert Hoover Lloyd, to typing class, where Miss Adeline timed us as we typed, or to the science classroom/laboratory of Mr. James Hester Hammonds, the emphasis was always the same—buckle down and do the work. You are here to learn.

The agricultural/shop classes were not held in the same building as the other classes. A large cinder-block building at the eastern side of the school property was the domain of Mr. Tom Blanks. A young and soft-spoken teacher, his classes were extremely popular with the male students, and understandably so. The subject matter was about farming methods, care of farming equipment, and how to construct things that were needed on farms. This was knowledge that had meaning then and could be used in a practical way.

Miss Artie Emanuel's home-economics classroom was a busy and popular one for many of the female students. The required freshman class focused on the knowledge and skills needed to plan and prepare nutritious meals and to set tables according to proper etiquette, as she called it. Students were expected to learn how to use a pattern and to sew a garment that was constructed well enough to wear.

Cooking was of interest to me, but sewing required more patience and precision than I had. It didn't take long for me to realize that getting a job that paid enough to buy clothes would be a necessity. If I didn't, then I would be poorly clothed for the remainder of my life. Miss Artie agreed with me.

One of my favorite places in high school was not a classroom, but the library. Miss Mary Martin Bell—tall, pretty, and elegantly attired—began her career as librarian at Magnolia in 1955, the same year I was a freshman. Always smiling and helpful to anyone who went to the library with a serious purpose, her demeanor could change with light-ning speed when she heard loud talking, laughing, or other behavior she found inappropriate in the library.

While our high school teachers were all business when it came to the classroom, they were equally excited and competitive when it came to the basketball season (both boys' and girls' teams), coached by Mr. Ned Sampson. A gentle giant of a man, Mr. Ned was a legend in the world of college basketball. It was said he could have played at any college, anywhere in the country, had he been white.

In the 1920s, the Robeson County Indian High School Athletic Conference was formed because Indian schools were not allowed to be part of conferences that included white schools. During my high school years, the four Indian high schools were located in Pembroke and the communities of Prospect, Saddletree, and near Fairmont. The rivalries were long held and the basketball games fiercely played.

The culmination of the season and highlight of the year was the Indian schools' basketball tournament, held in the gymnasium of Pembroke State College. No matter which school ultimately won the boys' or girls' championships, conversations about the games among students and adults alike alluded to cheating referees, money being given to certain officials, and how each school that failed to win should have won. Always, the hope was that next year, both trophies would come home to Magnolia.

The other big athletic event was Field Day, a competition of Robeson County Indian school students that was also held on the campus of Pembroke State in the spring. It was an all-day affair that focused on folk dances, spelling bees, and musical competitions for grades four through eight. High school students competed in outdoor events such as track and the javelin throw. Preparation took place during the fall and winter in physical-education classes, except for a few high school events, which held practices after school. If a student needed transportation home after school, Mr. Ned was often the driver.

Magnolia High School had many talented athletes, some of whom excelled in a specific sport, such as the javelin throw, while others were multifaceted athletes who excelled in a variety of sports. One such athlete was a young woman whom I came to know and admire.

Mary Lois Lowry was an attractive young woman who was a few years older than me. With very dark hair, eyes that lit up like twinkling stars, a slim body with an ample amount of femininity, and a desire to win at all that she did athletically, she was a natural athlete. She quickly became one of Mr. Ned's star female basketball players.

When she married Roscoe Burnette, a young man who was in the army and the son of family friends (Roscoe's father, Mr. Jim Burnette, was a member of the Magnolia School Committee), many people were distressed that Mary Lois would no longer be a student and that her athletic prowess would be missed. To the delight of many, Mary Lois continued high school and brought honor to the school as a member of the basketball team as well as with victories in many track events at the annual Field Day competitions.

I was glad not only for that reason but also because my parents allowed me to ride to and from Field Day with her. The freedom to celebrate with more adult rituals than we were allowed on the school buses was a bonus. My parents wouldn't have approved had they known.

Winning points for an event counted in a final tally to determine who won the Field Day competition. I could not tell you if Magnolia School ever won the trophy for any year I attended, but I can say with certainty that it was a day filled with rivalry, fun, and no homework. My mother was responsible for much of the planning and administrative coordination of the event in her position as the supervisor of Indian education for Robeson County. She was extremely glad each year when Field Day ended and was deemed a success.

*O*ur high school teachers had the best of intentions. They worked hard to teach us. But they did so with huge obstacles, some of which were insurmountable at the time. No doubt the biggest obstacle our teachers faced was the number of days many students missed in a typical school year, especially in the spring and fall. Because most of the students came from families that farmed, especially as tenants or sharecroppers, every available body and pair of hands was needed to prepare the fields and plant and hoe crops in the spring. There were also gardens that had to be planted and cared for; by the time school started in the fall, there was still tobacco to be cropped, graded, and tied and rows of cotton to be picked by hand.

Many high school students, and a few middle school students, spent many long days doing these chores instead of attending school. For most of them, it wasn't a choice but a necessity. The meager money people made from farming was the main income source for many families, as few other job options were open to Indians because of the legal segregation and discriminatory practices that were a reality in Robeson County at that time.

Given the need for help on farms and the general lack of other employment opportunities, a high school education was not a priority for many of the parents of students at Magnolia School. Students who had high absentee rates often had failing grades and weren't promoted to the next grade level. That situation resulted in many students, especially boys, being considerably older than their classmates. Some people called these young male students "man-boys." Physically developed, socially aware, and educationally deficient, they often dropped out before the rest of their classmates entered high school. The teachers, and both of my parents, understood this dilemma and were dismayed by the high dropout rate. It was a serious problem that seemed to have no solution.

Another issue was the heartbreaking problem of hungry students in grades one through twelve at Magnolia and other Indian schools in Robeson County, one of the poorest of all one hundred counties in North Carolina.

"How can anyone expect children of any age to learn when they're hungry?" my father asked rhetorically over and over again. "With a growling belly, the focus is not on what's in books. It's the need to eat."

When the federal government began to provide surplus foods to schools with large numbers of children living in poverty, both my parents were overjoyed. Free lunches were provided to many students; for many kids, according to my dad, their lunches at school were the first meal of the day. Miss Eunice Hammonds and her staff began their work early; they had long days preparing and serving meals that were nutritious, if not always the first choice of some of us.

It was not surprising that, with so many students whose parents had little in the way of financial resources, some students had few clothes, and some wore shoes that barely covered their feet or were the wrong size. This concerned my dad.

A large Converse plant in Lumberton manufactured tennis shoes of all sizes. Working with the management of this company, my dad arranged to have seconds donated to the school, and he used a small area in the principal's office to house the "shoe closet." From this tiny space, shoes were given to students of all ages, with a minimal amount of attention drawn to the need of the students receiving them.

For example, teachers were asked to quietly look for students in their classrooms who needed new shoes. Then, they were told to find something that a child who needed shoes had done well so that he or she could be rewarded—with a pair of tennis shoes. If students had not done anything of note—whether in the classroom, on the playground, to assist the teacher in some way, or to serve as a model for other students—then teachers were encouraged to promote that kind of activity so that the students wouldn't think they'd been given the shoes because they were poor.

As principal, my dad often stood in the hall during the changing of high school classes and roamed through the cafeteria during lunch hour. While most students believed this was a way to encourage good behavior (and it was), it was also a way of determining who needed new shoes. As the principal, my dad asked a few students to perform tasks for him and then gave them a pair of shoes as a gesture of his appreciation for a job well done. My dad always hoped the students never knew his real motive.

Some teachers talked about another obstacle they faced: a shortage of textbooks. How widespread that was, I don't know, but I do recall some students throughout elementary and high school not having a complete set of textbooks. Those students were often the ones who were frequently absent in grades three through eight.

The quality of the textbooks remained basically the same throughout my school years at Magnolia. Most of our textbooks were older ones, as evidenced by the names and dates of issuance recorded on a page near the front of the book, and some of the books were shabby. It was rare to use a new book, and having one's name be the first one on the user page was considered very special. Our teachers instructed us to treat new books with special care, or else we would have to pay a fine in May when textbooks were collected and examined for damage.

What I didn't know till later was that a 1935 North Carolina law stated that "Books shall not be interchanged between the white and colored schools, but shall be continuously used by the first race using them." Whether this law was followed completely is unclear, but it is perfectly clear that the state's intent was to keep not only the people of Robeson County segregated but the tools of learning as well.

Another negative factor for a large number of Magnolia School students was the distance they lived from school. Many students of all ages stood daily by the side of a dark road waiting for the school bus to pick them up for a ride of fifteen to eighteen miles. The ride home ended for some students as the sunlight was fading; for the student drivers, all of whom were more than glad to have this opportunity to earn money, the day was even longer.

Many of the teachers at Magnolia also began their days early, as they lived in or near Pembroke, twenty miles from their teaching jobs. But I never heard of a teacher who complained about the early hours or the demands of commuting to Magnolia. And why would they? In addition to liking their jobs, teachers were among the highest-paid Indians in Robeson County. No teachers I knew wanted to lose their jobs or jeopardize their future employment opportunities.

Though the students, faculty, and staff at Magnolia School faced daily challenges that were dismaying and even discouraging, the teachers and staff never allowed obstacles to keep them from caring about us and teaching us what they knew. Some say that the extra care we were given and the high expectations that were placed on us motivated some students to exceed beyond many people's expectations.

A long with the state laws that demeaned and discriminated against Indians in the state, the structure of Robeson County government was such that Indians had little, if any, clout or input into major decisions that had an impact on our daily lives. The Robeson County School Board of Education was, in many people's opinion, the worst example of this.

Five towns in Robeson County had their own school system and residents of each town elected a local school board. County residents not living in towns voted for members of the Robeson County School board. What created major problems for those of us living in communities, not towns, was that all town residents were also allowed to vote for members of the Robeson County School Board. This discriminatory pattern of voting, called "double-voting," ensured that no Indians were members of the Robeson County School Board while I attended public school.

The situation was further complicated by the fact that the county schools had separate schools for blacks, whites, and Indians, while the town schools had schools for blacks and whites but none for Indians. Indian children who lived in any of the five towns that had black and white schools attended Indian schools in the county. The exception was Pembroke, where the majority of students were Indians and the Pembroke schools were part of the Robeson County school system.

The sad reality was that there wasn't an advocate on the board of education for Indians. As a result, Indian children's educational needs were a low priority. Indians' educational progress was thwarted by racism.

Efforts to have the state legislature change this blatant discrimination were futile. A lawsuit filed by Janie Maynor Locklear against the

North Carolina Board of Elections, under the provisions of the Voting Rights Act of 1965 and appealed to the US Fourth Court of Appeals, finally ended this practice in 1975.

The Robeson County Board of Education hired a new supervisor of Indian schools in 1951, and the new Indian employee quickly made a disturbing discovery. The woman who held a similar position and responsibilities for white schools refused to share an office with her and the white supervisor also refused to share any information about the job duties or resources needed to perform the job. After the Indian supervisor discussed the situation with the superintendent of the Robeson County schools, she was given a private office and a few details about her job duties.

It was years later when I learned of the unfriendly reception my mother received when she went to work as the supervisor of Indian schools in Robeson County. It was later still when I was told that the white supervisor's husband was a prominent attorney in Lumberton who had close ties to the social and political leaders of the county. No one ever told me that racism had caused my mother's difficult early years of work for the Robeson County Board of Education. I figured that out by myself.

Robeson County was not the ideal place to be a student in the 1950s, and this was especially true for Indians. The challenges that Indian administrators, teachers, staff, and students faced were large and lasted far too long. That is always true when the challenges and obstacles are based on racism. But neither the challenges and hardships nor the second-rate status many people assigned us kept us from learning reading, 'riting, 'rithmetic, and right manners.

The power of education, the principal of Magnolia School told me over and over, would be the downfall of racism. So I studied hard and believed he was right.

Blessed by Boone

"Lena," my dad said, "would you like to go to Boone with your mother and go to school?"

It was a simple question, and I gave him a simple response: "Yes, I'd like that."

My answer took little thought and no time. On that late-fall day in 1951, I had no idea of the significance of either the question or the answer.

At the time, I was a thin, tall-for-my-age, dark-caramel-skinned ten-year-old girl in Miss Ophelia Thomas's fifth-grade class at Magnolia School. That my school was one for Indian students created no questions for me; the fact that my teachers were almost always Indians was as natural as afternoon recess.

What was of concern in my little world was that several boys in my class used handheld mirrors to see parts of girls' clothing that were private. Miss Ophelia never caught them misbehaving. I hoped that this bad behavior wouldn't occur in Boone. Surely, boys in town would have better manners than my country schoolmates.

We went to Boone for Mama to take some graduate courses at Appalachian State College. Both she and my dad were studying to earn their master's degrees in education. At the time, Appalachian was one of the few public institutions that offered graduate degrees, if not the only place in North Carolina, that Indians could attend.

My mother and I arrived in the mountain town of Boone in March, in the midst of winter. I was certain that we had traveled to the North Pole instead. Icy tree limbs swayed in the distance, and where the ground should have been was a white carpet of snow. As I got out of Mama's car, my breath was visible and threatened to freeze the tip of my nose. The howling of the Watauga County wind greeted us long before our hosts opened the door to our new home.

Mama had made arrangements for us to board with Doug and Ruth Redmond and their daughter Carol, who was also in the fifth grade. Their home on Oak Street was a large brick structure, and its backside on the first floor mostly consisted of large glass windows. From the high perch of the Redmond home, Boone's hospital and several of the college buildings were visible.

The Redmonds lived on the first floor, and college students lived on the second floor. Our room had two single beds, a sink, a hotplate, a desk, and two chairs. A bathroom used by three or four boarders, including us, was across the narrow hall from our room. The Redmonds agreed that we could have kitchen privileges for breakfast and dinner. After looking around that March Sunday, I was convinced that 209 Oak Street would qualify as a small mansion.

Nervousness didn't strike early on Monday morning. It wasn't until my mother parked the car and we began the walk to my new school that the butterflies began their dance in my stomach. The closer we got to the entrance, the more I became sure that it wasn't butterflies. I knew that I had one of those bugs that made stomachs hurt. I walked on, for my mother hadn't slowed down. She didn't seem to notice my distress.

Boone Demonstration School seemed large for an elementary school. It was a solid-looking building, and at least that was good, I decided. The howling winds probably wouldn't hurt it. Only my far-from-home Robeson County body would freeze, and that might happen any minute.

As we approached the school, I noticed children helping to direct traffic and assisting other students in crossing the street. Their yellow badges and suspender-like contraptions across their shoulders were a bit odd looking. I didn't have enough time to examine this in detail, for very quickly Mama opened the wide door, and we were inside the school. My eyes were wide open, and my heart pounded. I could see dozens of children in the hall, some walking and others just standing around. I thought some of them were looking at me. A couple of students were pointing fingers in my direction. My stomach began to hurt even worse. I could be at home headed to Miss Ophelia's class. Nobody pointed fingers at you there except the teacher.

Soon my mother was talking to a man who had a gentle, firm voice. I heard him say, "Mrs. Epps, we're delighted to have Lena here. I know she'll enjoy our school. Miss Walker and her class are waiting for her. I'll take you there."

That sounded more inviting than what I'd seen so far. I followed Mama and the man down the wide hall. My guess was that he was the principal of the school. We'd barely begun our walk when a boy about my height walked over to me and asked, "Are you the Indian? Do you scalp people?" The principal stopped, turned his head slightly, and reached back and touched my shoulder and said, "Of course she doesn't. What a silly idea. Now, head on into your class."

Stunned by the ignorance of the question and the sensitivity of the response, I walked quietly with my eyes on the floor. I vowed not to cry, but the tears that formed apparently hadn't heard the silent promise I made to myself. I was afraid of what might happen next. My desire to be here had vanished in about five minutes.

Miss Walker greeted us warmly and introduced me to the class. She mentioned how wonderful it was to have an American Indian in her class. She led me to a desk and suggested that I would enjoy the book she handed me. By the time my escorts had left, I was happily lost in the pages of a book. Later, some of the students invited me to eat lunch with them and made sure I was involved in recess activities. Miss Walker's class would be fine, even though I was still cold.

I did get some prolonged stares during my first days of school. But soon the stares stopped, or I forgot to notice them. No unkind words reached my ears after the first day. School days were filled with reading, math, geography, English, spelling, and whatever else Miss Walker planned for our class. Soon I was wearing the weird yellow suspenders and was honored to be a member of the school's safety patrol. I was away from home, but I felt at home there very quickly.

True to Mama's word, I did walk to school. Snow-covered ground and bitingly cold winds were often part of the walk. Sometimes Carol and I walked together; other times I walked to and from school alone. Either way had its own special benefits. With Carol there was always laughter and people, whether we went straight home from school or dawdled on the way. She attracted boys easily, and I watched in awe and envy as she flirted, and I listened in amazement as she planned who her next boyfriend would be. Her skills with both boys and her parents were far more sophisticated than any I'd yet encountered. She had the ability to get mostly whatever she wanted, especially getting out of practicing the piano. But I knew better than to even think of trying any of those techniques on Mama or boys. Being in Boone didn't change my mother's expectations of my behavior one bit.

Though my behavior didn't change, my options for after-school activities had been altered, and they increased dramatically. One of my favorites was going to the Boone Drug Store, after I survived the stress and apprehension of my first visit. On the way there, my mind replayed scenarios of Indians being asked to leave drugstore counters in Lumberton when they attempted to buy refreshments. That humiliation was nothing I wanted there or here. My heart was hammering as I sat down the first time at the counter with my new friends. The surprise and relief I felt when nothing happened but to get a Coke placed in front of me was a wonderful event in my life.

It didn't take long for visits to the drugstore to become a frequent part of my routine. Whether I went with Carol or other friends, our after-school time there was marked by laughter and fun. With no hesitation, we seated ourselves at the barstools and bought whatever we could afford, usually a fountain drink. Sometimes we pooled our resources and shared in the delight of an ice-cream float or a small sundae. Often I listened to my new friends talk about who liked who. I had nothing to contribute in those conversations, for I still thought of boys mostly as pests. Besides, I knew that no one liked me in "that way." What I did know was that I liked being connected to a group of people who treated me with consideration and respect.

Sometimes I met my mother at the College Book Store, a campus favorite for students and faculty. I'd have a Coke while my mother sipped coffee, and we'd talk about our day and her plans for my evening. Watching the people and straining to catch bits of their conversations about tests, dates, sporting events, and research papers was almost like attending a movie. I often wondered how I'd gotten so lucky to be there. I wondered if any of my Magnolia classmates could even imagine what my life in Boone was like.

Even going to church was a different and pleasant experience. The preacher at the Baptist church on Main Street didn't yell and terrify me with descriptions of my body burning in hell. Nor did he work himself into such a fervor that I feared his veins would pop as he preached. And having *fun* at church was a concept I'd never considered. I was not at all sure that the Boone youth group would be accepted in Robeson County, for we laughed a lot and learned very little. To my surprise, the adult leaders seemed to expect nothing more of us. And that wasn't a problem. I was in Boone.

Though I enjoyed school, my new friends, downtown Boone, and the church youth group, they paled in comparison to my real love in Boone. Like many loves of old, some of its features are blurred now. I do remember that it was a large brick building with wide, curving steps across its front. It held treasures that entranced me. The extraordinary acts of ordinary people thrilled me, as did the phenomenal discoveries of those who explored and persevered. The delights and woes of love came alive in my mind. The possibilities I read about became mine. The Appalachian State College Library was my special place. Both the books and staff became cherished friends.

What happened in that little mountain town came so quickly and felt so natural that I could hardly believe this was happening to me. It was an unexpected gift of freedom to be myself as I was. I, an American Indian girl, could enjoy the little things in life without fear of scorn or shame. I was free to walk wherever I wanted, with whomever I chose or whoever chose me. I could buy a soft drink and sit at the drugstore counter without fear of being asked to leave. I could explore ideas and learn in a place where I would never in my entire life be able to read all the books. I could now dream about the future with the certainty that it could come true. I loved life in Boone.

The winter snows finally changed to slush, and the harsh winds softened with the hint of warmth. I knew that blades of green, however small, meant spring was near. Soon I would return to the flatlands of my homeland, but a piece of my heart would remain high in the hills of Boone.

Someday, somewhere, I would find a place like Boone to live when I became an adult. I would live in that place where others would be glad I was me. My dream had become a reality. That was the blessing of Boone.

Friends and Fun

Friends were an important part of my life in high school, but I never had a wide circle of either female or male close friends. Attending a very small high school meant that everyone knew one another, but the fact that all but maybe two dozen of the student body rode buses to school prevented after-school visits with friends. Another factor was that many of my classmates were expected to work on the farms their parents tended or owned once they arrived home. Others performed household tasks and supervised younger siblings, assignments that I also did. Leisure time after school was not part of my world.

Another factor in having few close friends could have been how some of my classmates felt about me. Early in my freshman year, two female classmates told me, to my face, that I was stuck-up. That meant that I thought and acted as if I were better than my classmates. Quickly and sincerely, I denied this allegation.

"Never, ever did I think I was better, in any way, than anyone else," I told my classmates, "and I don't believe I ever acted that way toward you or anyone else."

What I didn't tell them was that I knew that if I ever behaved in a manner that caused others to feel devalued, and my parents heard about it, I would be in trouble. One of my parents, probably Mama, would talk long and hard about *all people being God's children* and the absolute necessity of treating every human being with respect and politeness. This was what God expected and Mama and Daddy required, she would say. On this point and at that time, I was much more concerned with Mama and Daddy's approval than that of God.

In my first year of high school, I was not particularly talkative. I watched, listened, and learned from my classmates. Who and what was popular? Which boy liked which girl, and vice versa? Who was seen at the Old Foundry, the favorite hangout for most Indian students I knew, on Saturday night? Who was talking to whom in the halls? To me, these were important things for a high school freshman to know.

What most people didn't know about me, and I shared with no one, was that I was much more comfortable with one or two people than a large group. So while I was without a large group of best friends, I did have a few friends whom I spent time with and had fun.

When I entered high school, I was not quite fourteen years old—younger than most of my classmates—and my parents were stricter than most other parents. At least that's what I thought. So in early high school, my social life was limited. Any excursions I took to the local Indian hangout and to high school basketball games away from our school were with female classmates who had driver's licenses or had sisters who did. No matter what the occasion or the ages, the young women had to be absolutely trustworthy and have good judgment and high morals in the opinion of my parents.

The Bell sisters not only fit my parents' high standards but were also blond, good-looking, and popular. Glennis was a sophomore when I was a freshman, and Toni and Catherine, her sisters, were seniors. Any time spent with the Bell sisters was fun, but Sunday afternoons were special when we went to the Old Foundry.

Located in the west end of Lumberton, the Old Foundry was a two-story building that offered drive-in food service, a room with large glass windows and barstools for casual eating, a dining room for meals, and an upstairs room for private parties. Owned and operated by the Oxendine brothers—Hubert, Heaverd, and Hilton, Indian businessmen who lived in Lumberton—it was the only restaurant in town where Indians could be seated and served inside.

During the week, customers at the Old Foundry were mostly adults. On Sundays, after church, some families came to eat Sunday dinner in the dining room. Later, on Sunday afternoons, the folks who arrived were primarily Indians of high school and college age who lived in or near Lumberton, the Saddletree community, and as far north as St. Pauls, a small town about fourteen miles away. No matter what the reason for visiting the Old Foundry on Sunday, most people dressed well. Many of us wore exactly what we'd worn to church earlier.

Getting to the Old Foundry on Sundays usually involved Toni and Glennis and me laughing and talking nonstop on the seven-mile trip into Lumberton. Their sister Catherine joined us sometimes, but most Sundays she was with one of her many boyfriends. Often, Toni took the long way to our destination as she drove slowly down Elm Street, the main street in Lumberton. Glennis and I became adept at doing two things simultaneously. We learned how to keep our eyes glued to the sidewalks and to scan the cars parked on both sides of the street. It was important to know who sat in the parked cars as well as who might be ambling along on the sidewalks. With practice, we became experts at spotting people we knew…or thought we'd like to know.

Just before we reached the fire station, Toni would make a right turn, and we'd cross the Fifth Street Bridge. By the time I was in high school, I no longer thought of snakes and bodies floating in the Lumber River. I thought about who I might see at the Old Foundry.

After parking the car and ordering something to drink, we'd sit in the car and talk, laugh, and look at the steady stream of cars bringing more people to join this Sunday-afternoon ritual. Toni was forever the matchmaker and wasted no time in practicing her craft.

"Look at him, Glennis," she said. "What do you think? Isn't that Alice's brother who's in the service now?"

"Hush, Toni. You know he likes Annie."

Laughter filled the car, and the routine continued: looking, sipping, talking, laughing, and looking.

Occasionally, another classmate joined us or went with us on this jaunt. Alvia Bolin, a dark-haired bombshell and classmate of Glennis, attracted attention wherever she went. Toni made certain this continued as she called to one of her male friends who walked by. "Look at her! Isn't she good-looking?" Toni said, nodding toward Alvia.

With his slightly bulging eyes and his muttering of something that we couldn't quite decipher, we knew he was impressed. It was Toni at her best, and I enjoyed watching and listening to her "cook something up," as Glennis and I called it. That was almost as much fun as watching the dozens of cars full of young people arrive.

Sometimes, Sunday afternoons brought other groups to the Old Foundry. Indians, primarily young men, came from other areas, including Pembroke. Tryon Lowry, my tall, good-looking cousin, and some of his friends, including Jerry Cummings, showed up occasionally. Always dressed to perfection and driving shiny late-model cars, they were handsome and had no dates with them. As much as I hoped they would, not one of the Pembroke boys ever asked me out for a date.

Flirting was perfected to an art form at the Old Foundry on Sunday afternoons. A glance of the eye, a quick introduction by a friend, or a special smile and hello from someone you knew, and a possible romance began. Whether anything would develop was unknown. What mattered most was the fun and excitement then and there at the Old Foundry.

A few young white men did come to our hangout. Some were from Lumberton, and a few came from as far away as Elizabethtown. Infrequently, someone made a comment about the presence of "white boys" being at our hangout, but I didn't see or hear about any altercations as a result. A few white soldiers from Fort Bragg sometimes appeared, and they had no need to try to disguise their military status.

The cropped hair and, in many instances, the strange-sounding accents were giveaways.

Flirting between Indian girls and white boys did happen, and dates were made and kept as well. At least that's what I was told. But for most of the people I knew, interracial interactions were limited by the community customs and practices of separation of the three races. It was, in most cases, hardly worth hearing family and friends saying, "You're trying to be white." We also heard the dire warnings about the dangers involved in interracial encounters, which often followed the accusation and taunt of "trying to be above your own race."

The parents of some of my classmates were very explicit: "Do *not* mingle with or date anyone other than Indians." That was enough to greatly limit the social interactions of many Indians, because most of the young Indian people I knew obeyed their parents. My parents never said a word about this.

Basketball was the only competitive sport Indian high schools had, and after the games, Magnolia High School students went to the Old Foundry. Dates, groups of teenage boys and girls, and some teachers might be spotted in their cars or at one of the booths or on the barstools inside. The basketball players stopped by for food and socializing as well. Sometimes, a container of homemade wine was passed around certain cars.

Students and supporters of rival schools were not very welcome on the nights Magnolia School had a basketball game or school event. Sometimes, these rivalries led to parking-lot scuffles and fights, which usually ended with the appearance, and at the strong suggestion, of one of the Oxendine brothers, who understood that good behavior was good for business. Most of us young people understood that, too, and behaved accordingly.

But whether it was after basketball games, Sunday afternoons, dates, or other occasions, my time at the Old Foundry was fun, plain and simple. Nothing out of the ordinary—it was where young Indian people could gather and be accepted as we were. And that, in itself, was extraordinary at the time.

Long before I started dating, I made a decision that was an important one regarding romance. For me, there would be no going steady. The idea of always going on dates with the same person seemed boring. And it seemed that only spending time with one person meant that it was not just about fun but was in fact very serious. I'd heard classmates and older girls talk about getting married, and marriage didn't interest me at all then.

But the deep honest truth about my having no interest in going steady was what three older high school girls who were going steady told me. They talked openly about "doing it." Though I was young and sheltered from many things, I knew that meant having sex. And there was no way that I would be doing it. My mother's words about young girls getting pregnant and the trauma and turmoil that caused for the girl and her family were firmly embedded in my brain. No boy was worth all that.

From years earlier, Grandmother Lela's comments about what all boys wanted came to mind. Her solution to solving the problem of unmarried girls getting pregnant was simple. Her advice was, "Keep your legs crossed at all times."

Later in high school, I did date some, but not nearly as much as many of my classmates. I decided there were several reasons why. Most obvious was that not many young men asked me out, and others were reluctant to ask me out because my dad was the principal of the high school we all attended. While I laughed at that reason, I realized Daddy's no-nonsense approach as a principal could be intimidating, especially to a young man interested in dating his daughter. And there was that early curfew. But the real reason, I believed, was that many of my female classmates had more appealing appearances and personalities. I accepted this without remorse, regret, or even much thought.

When I did have dates, most were with Indian boys from my high school. Going to basketball games, movies, and the Old Foundry were our most frequent destinations. We went to a few parties, always in a building far away from most other structures and adults. It was at these parties where dancing and the drinking of beverages other than soft drinks were common. Beer and wine were kept discreetly in cars, as was anything stronger, either commercially prepared or locally made.

The music was loud, and the dancing was nonstop. Since I always had an earlier curfew than the others, and my parents would likely be awake when I got home, I drank very little of anything alcoholic. I knew it would be in my best interest to be walking straight, talking politely, and doing nothing that would make my parents suspect that I hadn't been to a movie or to the Old Foundry.

In our senior year, Glennis and I sometimes rode to St. Pauls, the small town near where she and her family lived. We sometimes stopped at the Santee, a restaurant that had drive-in service and was operated by white people. We had a soft drink and surveyed who was in the other cars. It was there where I met several young white men who were friendly and handsome. We talked a lot and sometimes rode around town with one another. That didn't take long, but it was fun.

Among the few dates I had with white boys, I saw two boys more than once or twice. One was a young man who delivered the *Robesonian* to our home, and the other was from the St. Pauls area. Though my parents didn't know these young men personally, I guessed that my dad felt safe in my going out with both because he knew how to reach both of the boys and their parents. The *Robesonian* had a public telephone, and the other boy's father was a successful and well-known farmer in his community.

Truthfully, the dates with the white boys were somewhat awkward. Both the young men and I knew that going to Lumberton or St. Pauls to a movie in the town theaters would not be a good option. Seated in the upstairs balcony could be an invitation for hard stares and mean comments. And there was the possibility of worse responses, such as stolen hubcaps, smashed windshields, slashed tires, or spirited fights. As a result, much of the time we went to those drive-in movies or drive-in cafés that accepted both Indians and whites around Lumberton or St. Pauls. Sometimes we went to Fayetteville. It seemed that people took less notice of interracial couples there.

In mid-January of 1958, when I was a senior, I had a date with the boy from St. Pauls. When I told my mother about it, her face took on a very serious look. When I asked her what was wrong, she replied: "A Ku Klux Klan rally is scheduled for near Maxton tonight, and we hear that some of our Indian men plan to be there. It'll probably get ugly and be dangerous there. So, whatever you do, stay away from Lumberton, Pembroke, or that area. Do you understand what I'm telling you? Stay away from Lumberton and Pembroke."

She didn't have to reiterate the dangers of a Klan rally with Indian men planning to attend or intervene. My date and I headed north on Highway 301 and spent the evening in Fayetteville. Even there, I was nervous and more than glad to be home safely, long before my curfew.

Spring came, our yearbooks arrived, and my classmates and I scribbled notes and good wishes to one another. Quickly, graduation day arrived, and Glennis and I headed to White Lake, a popular place with clear water, amusements, food and about 25 miles away, to celebrate. High school was history.

While many people remember high school dating and group activities as being among their most treasured life memories, that wasn't my experience. I had too few dates and too few places to actually go and do anything fun to create a head full of treasured memories; my high school social life was scarce and simple. But it was real. More than anything, I was always grateful for the few people who were close friends and shared their time, transportation and laughter when we were in high school.

With enrollment in college, I spent less time in Saddletree and other parts of Robeson County. What increased was my awareness of just how few options I had for social activities at home. There were still movies and the Old Foundry, but no one called me for dates as I was accustomed to at college, and parties with dancing and loud music were largely absent. I missed the dates and the parties.

The exception to this was during the Christmas holidays. The rumor was that "Buddy" Bell (Glennis's older brother) and some of his Pembroke friends were the organizers of a large party at the Old Foundry. No one ever confirmed this, and it really didn't matter. What mattered was having a special event to attend while I was at home.

Getting to this room involved entering the main dining room and then climbing very narrow and winding steps that seemed to creak all the way to the second floor. The party room was rectangular in shape and not nearly large enough for the crowd of people jammed into it. Loud music blared from a phonograph, a steady stream of blurred voices created a muted buzz, and I heard lots of laughter. But the main thing was dancing. *Lots* of dancing! At times I thought I could feel the floor moving, not just my feet.

Those attending were primarily Indian people, college age and older. Sometimes I went with Glennis, and other times I went alone. Several people who had been my teachers in elementary and high school were there, as were many others from various parts of the county. The women dressed in semiformal attire, and the men wore coats and ties. It was the most sophisticated event, other than a wedding, I'd attended in Robeson County. And I loved it.

By this time, I was able to tell my parents that I was going to a party at the Old Foundry and that it would be late when I got home. They raised no objections. Had they known about the drinking and the number of people squeezed happily into that small space, they likely would have voiced some concerns. Besides the winding stairs on the inside, the other exit was a narrow and rickety metal stairway leading to the outside. Without a doubt, a fire marshal would have shut the party down. I always hated for those parties to end or when I had to leave… whichever came first.

In the summers of my early college years, I enjoyed going to South Carolina to dance a lot and drink a little. Glennis and several others, including her brother Pete, and I sometimes drove to the Dillon area, which had several juke joints, as they were called. What was inside these places I never knew, but they had jukeboxes in areas much like a covered patio outside the main buildings. There we could either buy a beer or drink one that we'd taken with us and dance the night away. Always, it was the dancing that made me the happiest.

Summers also found me spending time with Carolyn Sampson, a friend from Pembroke. We often cruised through Lumberton on Sunday afternoons and visited not only the Old Foundry but several white drive-in restaurants in the east part of town. But we were never brave enough to stop at the Lumberton Dairy Bar. Located on Pine Street, it was the place I believed to be the meeting place for the high school and college children of Lumberton's wealthy white residents. I was certain that we would be asked to leave, even if we just sat in our car. It was my plan to never have that happen again if I could avoid it.

Sometimes, Carolyn would arrange a date for me with young men who attended Pembroke State College. Our double dates with those young white men usually meant that we went to parties or nightspots in western Robeson County, near Maxton or Rockingham (in North Carolina) or McCall (in South Carolina), where beach music and current popular and soul music dominated. Carolyn had no curfew at home, and I often spent the night there. Parties lasted longer that way.

In the summer following my junior year at Meredith, I attended Pembroke State College and took a general chemistry class. On the very first day of that class, I met a tall, skinny, friendly young man with strawberry-blond hair and a smattering of freckles on his face. Curtis Hunter Jr. was from Lumberton, and he was white. He became my chemistry lab partner. After receiving failing grades on our first test, Curtis and I decided we would have some study sessions together. We began our study sessions on campus after classes, and then had some sessions at my parents' home.

We enjoyed each other's company, and it wasn't long before Curtis and I were hanging out. We did the usual Old Foundry and other drive-in café rituals. One of our favorite night activities was to go to the Lumberton airport, a favorite spot for dating couples, and drive by to see whose cars we recognized. He pointed out those of his white friends, and I did the same for Indian people I knew.

We often took soft drinks and snacks and had refreshments while driving through the maze of cars parked at the airport. Occasionally, a small bottle of liquor went with us, and we had mixed drinks at the "airport bar," our phrase for drinking and snacking while sitting in the car at the airport. When the mood struck, we'd turn the radio up and dance on a runway away from the other cars. During our time together that summer, we never drank to excess, never became romantically involved, and never encountered mean words or insults. (Or, if Curtis did, he never mentioned it to me.)

During the summer chemistry class, I met other white people who were friendly, polite, and fun. Jean Ramey, a pretty young woman from Lumberton who attended Peace Junior College in Raleigh, was the other white person I felt most comfortable with. I'm not sure which surprised me most: passing chemistry, even after causing a minor explosion in the chemistry laboratory, or making friends with white students. Both were important milestones for me.

That summer marked the first time I experienced hope for a future that included Indians and whites openly being friends in Robeson County. It was a welcome change from the total separation and segregation of Indians and whites that was so familiar to me. And it made me believe that the secret meetings and what I called "dark dates" (not being seen in daytime with whites, especially those of the opposite sex) might, one day, be a thing of the past.

Everyone wanted to have friends and fun. I knew this had to be true, because we were all people. One day, some day, I believed that skin color wouldn't make a difference in determining friends in Robeson County, or anywhere else. Until then, I would live as happily as I could… and dance as often as possible.

The Road to Raleigh

There was never any doubt in my mind that I would go to college. The benefits of acquiring as much education as possible were ingrained into my head by my parents from the time I was very young. They did not lecture me or aim directives at me. Rather, through their conversations with each other and with people outside our immediate family, the value of a college education was made perfectly clear to me.

What wasn't clear was where I would attend college. There were no high school counselors who could guide this process or talk with the thirty or so of us Indian students who would graduate from my small rural high school in late May of 1958. The sad fact is that guidance counselors were probably not necessary, for most of my classmates would likely continue to be tenant or sharecropping farmers, just as their parents were. A couple of the male graduates might enter military service, and a few of my classmates might leave Robeson County to seek work elsewhere. "Public work," our phrase for a job in a shop or store, could be an option for some. The small number who did go to college would likely attend nearby Pembroke State College.

Even though graduation was approaching in a couple of months, I felt no sense of urgency nor need for a decision to be made. My parents apparently shared my sense of having plenty of time, for they had not brought up the subject with me.

On a couple of occasions when someone inquired about my plans, I replied that I wanted to attend the University of North Carolina. Actually, my response was, "Chapel Hill." My parents said nothing until one day in early April, when my dad asked this question: "Lena, have you thought about attending Meredith College?"

His question surprised me greatly, for not once had I thought of Meredith College. "No, I haven't," I replied simply and with complete calmness.

What I knew about Meredith College was very little; it was an all-girls' college, as people called it, and it was in Raleigh. It didn't seem to attract the numbers of the very wealthy and socially prominent young women who were students at Saint Mary's College and Peace College, both junior colleges for women in Raleigh. This assumption was based on what I'd read in the local newspaper about where white girls were going to college. And yes, I did read that kind of thing, and I recognized several names as being those of various mayors, doctors, lawyers, and businessmen in Lumberton. But that really didn't bother me, because I was neither white nor wealthy.

At the time, I didn't think I knew anyone who had attended Meredith. But the idea was intriguing. I loved Raleigh, or at least what little I had seen of what many of us called the "capital city," and I was certain that going to college there would be exciting. After all, North Carolina State College was a short distance away, and most of the students were males! As an added bonus, Chapel Hill was in easy driving distance.

A week or so later, Daddy announced that he, my mother, and I would be going to Raleigh that day. He had business to attend to there, and he wanted me to see the Meredith campus. Neither Mama nor Daddy had given me any idea what to expect on this trip. And because they hadn't, I gathered that my job was to ride to Raleigh and wait for further instructions. Late in the afternoon, the three of us turned off Hillsborough Street and approached the Meredith College campus. It was a sight to behold for this rural Robeson County Indian girl!

A long driveway with huge expanses of well-manicured pastureland on either side led to a circular driveway that blended into another long driveway, which was the exit from the campus. Behind the circular driveway stood an impressive older brick building with Roman-type arches as the front facade. On the eastern and western sides of the circular drive were large contemporary brick buildings that I assumed were classroom buildings. After parking the station wagon near the western classroom building, my dad walked into the older brick building with arches. My mother and I sat in the car and waited for his return.

As we waited, and as I silently wondered what the nature of this visit was really about, I watched students as they came out of the two buildings that appeared to be classroom buildings. All carried books or book bags, and all sizes and shapes of college-age girls appeared. I noted that they all were white girls. That was no surprise. I hadn't really expected to see anyone with dark skin like mine.

Finally, after about forty-five minutes, we saw Dad as he exited the older building behind the circular drive and head toward us.

"So, what do you think, Lena?" Dad asked.

"I think it's a pretty campus," I replied.

"Well, Dr. Campbell, the president of Meredith, thinks it would be a good idea for you to visit the campus. If you like it, then we'll take the next steps."

I was delighted with the prospect of visiting the Meredith College campus and soon began counting the days till I would return for a visit. According to my dad, the visit would take place during the college's May Day weekend celebration, and that made it all the more exciting. Not a word more was spoken on our return trip home about what else Dr. Campbell had said, and I didn't ask.

Soon I was on my way to Raleigh again. This time I would spend the weekend. And what a weekend it was! Prospective students were assigned student hostesses for the visit, and we who were guests spent the two nights in the dorm room with our student hostess. We ate meals in the dining hall and, of course, talked about college life in general. Yes, the courses were hard, but not impossible. It was good to be at an all-girls school, they said; no guys were around to distract you when you had work that had to be done. And yes, the campus had a social life! Oh my, this sounded like heaven to me.

The May Day celebration took place on Saturday afternoon. The May queen and her court proceeded into the grassy quadrangle formed by four very old brick dorms and anchored on the south end by Johnson Hall, the building at the end of the long driveway leading to the college. Belk Hall, the college dining hall, anchored the northern end of the quadrangle. For quite some time, the May queen, the May court, and their escorts and all of us who attended watched a dance recital that included all kinds of dances, both contemporary and traditional. The maypole dance was the highlight. With the brilliant sunshine and sparkling green grass; the beauty of the May queen, her attendants, and their handsome escorts; and a rainbow of colors clothing the student body and guests, the whole scene seemed to be part of a Technicolor movie. I was certain that I was Alice and that I had stepped into Wonderland.

Not long after the ending of the May Day festivities, a tall, beautiful young woman approached me and asked if I had a date that evening. When I answered that I had no plans, she told me that her brother had asked her to arrange a date with him. She took me to a balcony on the dorm floor where I was a guest and indicated that the tall, handsome boy with the blue shirt and off-white slacks was her brother. Totally stunned and very pleased, I agreed that I would be ready for his call later in the evening.

The young Mr. Hight was movie-star handsome and a southern gentleman. With his friend and a date, we enjoyed a movie at the Ambassador Theater in downtown Raleigh. By the time we stopped for a Coke somewhere between downtown Raleigh and the Meredith campus, I was certain that Cinderella at the ball couldn't have been more enchanted than I was. A Meredith College girl? Oh yes, this is for me!

As my date and I approached Vann Dorm, where I was a guest, we saw many other couples returning from their Saturday-night activities. The breezeway, as I later learned it was called, was "good night" headquarters. Many looks and some blatant stares focused on my dream date and me. *No big surprise there*, I thought. I ignored them, smiled good night to Prince Charming, and simply floated up to my bed. This exceeded all my expectations and then some.

On Sunday morning, all the students and other guests and I attended the churches of our choice, arriving via city-owned buses whose drivers knew all the places of worship where Meredith Angels, as the school's students were called, attended. Soon after lunch, my mother picked me up, and she didn't have to ask how I'd enjoyed the weekend.

"Meredith is where I want to attend college," I told her.

She didn't ask questions about the weekend or ask why I'd made a decision so quickly. She smiled and simply said, "We'll see."

Soon after the Cinderella weekend, my dad told me that in order to attend Meredith, I'd have to take a test. "It's no big deal," he said. "Just go and do it and don't worry about it."

The fact that we had to drive to Wilmington, some ninety miles away, should have been a clue, but I was clueless. The plan was to go to Wilmington, arrive at 8:00 a.m. sharp, and get the test out of the way. Oh, and don't forget to take two number 2 pencils with erasers and the special identification badge that had been sent via Western Union and barely arrived the day before the test. Whatever it takes—let's get it done.

Early on that Saturday morning, I was slightly groggy from lack of sleep and nervous from not knowing exactly what to expect when my dad and I arrived at what he said was the proper place for the test. Surely, I thought, this couldn't be New Hanover High School; it appeared to be larger than Meredith College. As we walked into the building, and after Dad left after being assured that we were at the right place, I wondered if there were more to this than what he had told me. By now, my mental state was not calm, but neither was I totally overwhelmed with anxiety.

As I entered a classroom full of young people, I decided that all I could do was complete the test. Surely, it couldn't be that important. Or could it? No one paid any attention to me, which was good. Quite suddenly, as a very large young man with skin about the color of my own entered the room, the give-and-take of conversation began.

"Hey, Roman, how ya doing? Whatcha doing here? Big man, come on in!"

Obviously, this young giant was well-known and well-liked.

"This is my last chance," the young giant responded. "I gotta get this test score up so I can play ball at State."

Then and there, I knew that this test that "was no big deal" was important. And, as soon as I scanned the first page, I knew that either my dad didn't know much about this test or hadn't wanted to frighten me. Either way, this test would be different from any test I'd taken.

The first section was all about grammar, literature, and composition, and it was difficult. The final sections were about math and were impossible. The tests were so far beyond what I knew that I completed what little I could before anyone else finished. My hopes of becoming a Meredith student faded quickly. I knew what I had to do.

As soon as we got out of the busy Saturday traffic, I began my embarrassing confession. "Dad," I began, "we need to start making plans for me to attend another college."

"Why do you say that, Lena?"

"Because I failed that test," I replied. "I knew absolutely nothing on it, especially the math. I finished way ahead of everyone else. So, there goes Meredith College."

It was quiet for a second or two. And with no anger or disappointment in his voice, he spoke. "Don't worry about it too much, Lena. Things will work out."

His quiet confidence did nothing to bolster my faltering hopes. I knew with great certainty that when the fall came, I would attend Pembroke State College. Pembroke would accept me, because my mother was a graduate and she and her family were well-known by many in the town and on the campus. I didn't think there was a test to pass for admission. I hoped that those two factors would make it possible for me to get in there. I would live at home and commute; it would be much less expensive, I guessed. And I'd make some new friends. But Pembroke was not my first choice. Not anywhere close.

My dream was to live, learn, and be part of a place where I'd never lived before, a place with concerts, museums, restaurants, football games, and parties with loud music that I would attend and enjoy. I wanted to meet people whose backgrounds and heritages were totally different from those of the farming community in which I grew up. I longed for the freedom I thought would come with being away at college. Of course, college would have an abundance of good-looking men with good manners. But most important was my dream of studying and living in a place where my skin color would be accepted. I longed for my Indian heritage to be valued. But as the days passed without hearing a single word from Meredith, I felt my dream disappearing, quickly and quietly. All because of a test!

It was in mid-June when the letter arrived, and I was both excited and scared. Mostly, I was scared. How would I explain to the few people who knew that I wanted to attend Meredith College that I had failed to be admitted? How embarrassing it would be to confess that my test score was too low to get in. No one would ever believe it. I had a very high grade-point average. I was known as the brain in my class, even though I didn't believe that about myself. After the test in Wilmington, I knew that was not true.

Finally, I opened the letter and screamed…loudly. I got in! I got in! It was almost more than I could comprehend. Visions of parties, cute boys, a curfew later than my parents allowed, a nice roommate, and new clothes were all part of the kaleidoscope of the life I saw before me beginning in September. Going to the desk in my bedroom, I pulled out a piece of stationery and wrote my name and that of Meredith College, Raleigh, North Carolina, over and over again. The fact that going to classes and studying hard would be the most important part of this major change in my life would come later. For now, I smiled and laughed and started planning what I'd need to make the transition from high school in the country to college in the capital city.

My parents were happy for me, but theirs was a subdued joy. No shouts or cheers. No phone calls to share the good news with family or friends that I heard. But none of that surprised me; that would seem like bragging or showing off. Neither were part of my parents' makeup or behavior.

My summer continued as before my dream had come true: "handing tobacco" with a few high school classmates, boys and girls who had dropped out of school years ago, and an assortment of adults who had never heard of Meredith College. If it wasn't a "putting-in-tobacco" day, my mom often pressed me into service to help string beans or shell peas from the gardens of those who shared generously with her. There was always laundry waiting and the frequently irritating job of keeping an eye on the boys, who seemed to take great delight in doing the opposite of whatever I asked or suggested.

On one hot Saturday in mid-July, Glennis Bell, Alvia Bolin, and I headed to White Lake for a day of fun. It was there where we met several young soldiers who were stationed at Fort Bragg. Having graduated from college, they were several years older than the three of us. I lied and said I'd just finished my freshman year at Meredith College and would be returning there in September. When the young soldier from New York said he'd like to visit me in Raleigh, I knew that soon life would be good. This was yet another reason I was more than ready to get on the road to Raleigh.

Soon, July was over, and I learned that my Meredith roommate would be Betty Orr, a rising sophomore, from Mountain Home, a small town near Asheville. After we had discussed color schemes and Betty had given me some ideas about things I would need, my mother suggested that we go to Raleigh to shop. Our destination was the large Belk's store on Fayetteville Street. We selected and purchased two sets of twin sheets, a blanket and bedspread, three sets of brightly colored towels, and a trunk, clothes, and shoes.

The clothes we bought were unlike what I'd had in high school. We purchased matching sweater sets and wool skirts with silky linings for dates and special occasions and a couple of Sunday outfits, complete with the softest kid-leather gloves and beautiful leather pump shoes. New pajamas, underwear, and a bathrobe that was as soft and cuddly as a summer cloud were now mine to take to Meredith College. Again, I was Alice in Wonderland, but this was real.

The day before we made the ride to Raleigh to enroll me as a freshman student at Meredith, my mother came to my bedroom and found me sitting at my desk. Staring out the window, I was aware that my childhood was ending. Though I was not yet seventeen, I knew that my life would change once I became a Meredith College student. Both the security of my parents' love and the safety of their protective shelter from much of what was bad in life would be distant…even though I detested their rules and expectations about my social life. All of a sudden, I was afraid.

Mama stood at the door of my bedroom and looked at me without speaking. "What are you thinking, Lena?" she finally asked.

Uncharacteristically, I said nothing. Walking quietly to my bed, she sat down and spoke. "It's an exciting time for you, Lena. It's a scary time as well. That's how it should be. You're leaving home, and that's exciting. You're beginning college, and that's scary for anyone." She paused for a very long time, looked at me for an even longer moment, and began to talk again. "You're going to meet a lot of people who will like you."

And, as quick as a flash, I asked, "What about the people who don't like me? What about the people who don't like Indians?"

Without hesitation she replied, "There will always be people you won't like and people who won't like you because of different interests, personalities, and different upbringings. That's to be expected. As for those who don't like you because you're an Indian, there's not one thing you can do about them. If that's the case, just remember that not getting to know you because of who you are is their loss. Be friendly, be polite, and don't give them a second thought. Hold your head high, be proud of who you are, work hard, and move on. Everything will work out just fine."

I thought she'd finished, but she smiled that little smile reserved for special occasions when someone needed to know that she was there for them, even when doubt and fear were replacing a normal heartbeat of laughter and love of life. Mama spoke with a firm voice: "Your dad and I don't expect all A's from your college experience. We know that an important part of college is the social aspect of it. Your job will be to work hard in class and balance that with fun. That's what college is all about. Or that's what we hope it will be for you. We know you can do it, and we know you will."

With one more smile, she left the room as quietly as she'd entered.

Well, I hope you're right, I found myself thinking. *I do want to do well in college.* Good grades and good times. That's exactly what I want; that's exactly what I'll work for in college—Meredith College, that is.

My high school graduation gift, a matched set of Samsonite luggage, was packed, and the new trunk waited to be filled. My heart was calm, and my excitement was high. I was ready to get on the road to Raleigh.

Magnolia School Years-Photographs

Magnolia School, Highway 301, seven miles north of Lumberton

Lena, freshman in high school

High school classmates-front row: Louise Chavis, Alvia Bolin, Lena, Glennis Bell, Noyal Ann Hunt; back row: Ancie Dale Sampson, Catherine McGirt, Linda Gail Revels, Betty Lois Bell, Mattie Brewer, Joyce Woodell, Evie Emanuel

Lena, senior year

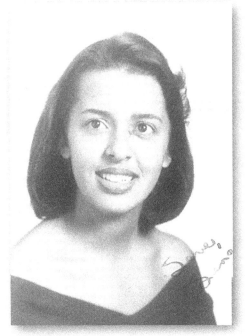

Lena, senior portrait

Cam, Lena (in senior year), Franklin

Glennis Bell, Archie Revels, and Lena at the junior/senior dinner-dance

Helen Locklear and Lena

Angel Years

Heaven Bound

The matched Samsonite luggage and large trunk waited, tightly packed, in the pink Rambler station wagon. In a zippered garment bag placed carefully on top of everything else was a long, white formal evening gown. My brothers promised to behave and follow the instructions of the person who would look after them until our parents returned in the late afternoon. Finally, my dad and mom and I were dressed and ready to begin the two-hour trip to Raleigh, where I would enroll as a member of the 1958 freshman class of Meredith College.

It was a hot day, with the sky the color people in North Carolina call "Carolina blue," and the sun dazzled so brightly that we needed sunglasses. As beautiful as the day was, and as excited as I was, I didn't talk much. Strangely, neither did my parents.

Perhaps they both had memories that were filling their heads. Was Mama reliving the day I was born? Was Daddy remembering how tiny I was at birth and how quickly I became a "little butterball"? Were they remembering how I followed Daddy's English setter, Old Bob, wherever he roamed? Or maybe they were remembering how I learned to read by asking about words on the corn-flakes box and how I loved going to first grade in Miss Mary's class.

No, I decided, they wouldn't think about when I was a baby or in elementary school. My guess was that they were thinking about the many times they had talked about the importance of education in my presence and their silent hope and expectation that I would go to college.

Whether those conversations had been at home between the two of them or with adult friends in other places, those conversations always focused on the value of a good education. They believed that education was vital for people of *all* skin colors to learn more about people and be more receptive to a variety of life experiences. A college education, they said, would help in the elimination of legal discrimination, provide more and better employment opportunities, open the door to a more fulfilling lifestyle, and enable one's children to have a better life.

In my heart, I knew my parents were pleased that the day had come when I would become a college student. But I guessed they probably had more than a few concerns about me. They knew they'd done the best they could to instill Christian values in me; they also knew that I was anxious to be away from home, have more freedom than they'd given me, and to live where there were more things to do. They likely remembered comments from family, friends, and acquaintances who reminded them of the possible dangers of a sixteen-year-old girl being away from home. They knew that I would prove or disprove that American Indians would have more freedoms in Raleigh than in Robeson County. If they had concerns, they didn't speak of them. Knowing my mother, she had prayed for my well-being. And Daddy? He'd try to keep his mind on the road.

Underneath my uncharacteristic silence, a well of emotions grew. The farther we traveled away from our home in the Saddletree community, the more my thoughts increased about the significance of this day. The anticipation of the remainder of this day, and days to come, made my heart beat quicker.

Surely, college girls were allowed to stay out past eleven. And certainly, I would have the freedom to date whomever I pleased without experiencing what I termed the "FBI investigation" into who the boy's people were and where his parents lived and then hear those questions repeated when my date arrived to pick me up. I knew their questions, comments, and rules were grounded in love, and I also knew that sixteen was not the legal age of an adult. But I had graduated from high school in three years, lived for short time periods away from my parents, and longed to be free of the limits set by segregation in my birthplace.

As we traveled north of Fayetteville, we passed the small grove of trees where our family had eaten many hot dogs on the trip to visit my dad's family in northern Person County. I hoped that those roadside picnics that happened because American Indians weren't allowed in restaurants and cafes were history. We drove through Lillington, and then quickly we passed through Fuquay-Varina. Soon, we approached Raleigh, also known as the Capital City of North Carolina. I sat up straight and took in as many sights and sounds as I could from my third of the crowded back seat, the only available space in the Rambler.

Circling the North Carolina State Capitol building, we drove west on Hillsborough Street past Saint Mary's Junior College, bars, shops, cafés, large old homes, and the NC State College bell tower. As we did so, an amazing thought surfaced. This was part of my new hometown—actually, only the second town I'd called home. Excitement bubbled quickly up to my face and produced a silent smile.

Yes, I was happy to be in Raleigh. I couldn't wait to be a college student, and I was excited about making new friends. But it was then when my heightened level of anticipation dimmed slightly. Would anyone want to be my friend? It would be obvious that I had dark-brown skin. *Well, idiot*, I thought to myself, *of course you do! You're an American Indian. It's not time to worry about that*, I told myself. *I'll be fine. Mama told me I would.*

Driving past fraternity houses and dorms on the campus of NC State, my apprehension disappeared and my anticipation increased. Thoughts of meeting many young men became my focus. Lots of young men. I knew we had almost reached our destination when the tantalizing smell of freshly baked bread filled the hot interior of our car, because a large commercial bakery was located across the street from the entrance to Meredith.

When Daddy slowed the car to a crawl and made a right turn, we entered the Meredith campus. Two long, tree-lined streets, with open meadows bordering both streets, was the picturesque scene that again greeted us. Separating the entrance and exit lanes was a wide, grass-filled berm. At the end of both streets stood the old but stately Johnson Hall, the administrative offices of the college.

Leaning forward in the back seat, I saw a line of cars traveling ever so slowly toward Johnson Hall. A backward glance revealed a similar scene. Like a small-town parade, cars of all makes and colors inched toward Meredith. From Manteo to Murphy and a few places beyond the borders of the Old North State, a nickname from the past for North Carolina, we moved closer to becoming students at Meredith. I hoped the student guides were right. They said being at Meredith was a bit of heaven on earth.

Trudging up to the second floor of Vann Hall with luggage and linens didn't resemble heaven at all. It was hard work getting up those flights of stairs. Add a bevy of daughters with parents trailing behind with full arms, and we had barely any room to move at all going up and down the steps. As my parents and I paused for a trio to pass, I'd say hello and sometimes offer what I thought was a welcoming smile. Occasionally, someone returned a smile; other times I received a cold, hard stare, most often from an adult with an incoming freshman.

That's not my problem, I'd think. *Not my problem at all.* Mama said this would likely happen, and my job was to be friendly and move on. And so I did—with a bit of apprehension, yes, but not enough to dim the excitement and wonder of my being there. I was there for orientation week, and my roommate, Betty Orr, was friendly and helpful. My business was to move into Vann Hall, not to worry about adults who thought about the brown color of my skin. On to moving in!

With my mom, Betty, and me working together, it didn't take long to unpack my belongings and make my bed. Daddy had disappeared into the unknown. I guessed he was outside, resting on a bench away from the young female voices whose nervous laughter bounced off the walls and down the long hall of the dormitory, the sound of two telephones ringing in unison, and the yell of "Jean or Jayne, the phone's for you!" The announcement, in a loud voice, of "man on the hall!" was surprising, but I quickly adjusted to it. I knew I wouldn't hear that phrase often...most likely only on moving days.

No, Lena, this is not Saddletree, I thought. *This is a different world. It's a world of whiteness. This is a world of white girls with many shades and hues of white skin, and they have many body shapes, including slim, overweight, and a few of the movie-star variety. We will eat whatever white people eat, and I hope our clothes will all be about the same. Quite a few of these white faces are smiling, yet they, too, are all different. Even the stares come in a variety of looks. All of this belongs here at Meredith. But Lora Evelena Epps*—my legal name and what my mother called me when she was really serious—*this is part of your world, too. And I am excited and glad to be here.*

Quicker than I'd imagined, my parents were preparing to leave my new world, a little piece of heaven in Raleigh, and return to Saddletree in the middle of Robeson County.

"Well, Lena, we'll take a walk around the campus with you, and then we'll be heading home," my dad said.

As the three of us walked across the quadrangle, I pointed out the Belk dining hall in the distance, and together we found the small post office and tiny student lounge. We ended up in a parking lot next to the familiar Rambler. I hesitated, unsure of what to do or say.

"Write us, Lena. Once a week," Mama said. "And we'll see you in October."

Nodding my head, I said OK and hugged both of them. A sense of sadness rose from somewhere deep within and startled me. *How can you be sad when you've waited so long for this moment*, I wondered. *You have so much to do, to see, to look forward to*, a little voice reminded me. That was true, I knew, but for no reason at all, tiny pangs of longing for Daddy and Mama touched my heartstrings, and I had the urge to ask them to stay. Just for a few minutes.

With a mixture of emotions I hadn't experienced before, I turned and walked quickly away from them and didn't look back. Ready or not, I had a new home, here and now at Meredith College. A new life awaited me. It was time for it to begin.

Faltering Angel

Ready to Fly

True to the tradition of my upbringing and a requirement of being a Meredith student, my first activity on the Sunday following orientation week was attending church. It came as no surprise that the majority of us chose Baptist churches located near downtown Raleigh or the college campus since Meredith was a Baptist-supported institution and many students were of the Baptist faith. The city buses that took us to church reappeared to return us to the campus that people often called the "Angel Farm."

With no wrinkles in our finest Sunday dresses, hose, and high-heel pumps, and many wearing or carrying gloves, we were the epitome of southern Sunday style. My mother would have loved to have seen us in our Sunday best. But even better, she'd say, Meredith girls went to church every Sunday. That we had no choice in the matter wouldn't matter to her one tiny bit.

Later that first Sunday afternoon, my roommate Betty reminded me that Sunday supper came in a brown paper bag. A sandwich, fruit, and something else light, as she described it, was the Meredith tradition for Sunday nights. *Fine*, I thought. Sunday-night suppers in Saddletree were often sandwiches or cold leftovers from Sunday dinner. But Betty suggested that we go downtown and have pizza at Gino's. She said it was the best in Raleigh.

I didn't tell Betty that I'd never eaten pizza. What I did tell her was that I'd love to go to Gino's. And so, for the second time that day, we rode the city bus downtown, got off near the church we'd attended earlier, and walked south on Fayetteville Street. As we came closer to Belk's, I could see a line of people standing still.

"Betty, why are all those people standing in line?" I asked.

"They're waiting to get inside Gino's," she told me. "It's a very popular place."

Once inside the dimly lit room, I was amazed to see so many people and to hear such a hubbub of voices. Young men, girls, couples, and families were all laughing, talking, and eating at tables with single wine bottles doubling as candleholders. Very quickly a waitress appeared to take our order. Not wanting to show my total ignorance about anything on the menu but spaghetti and salad, I ordered the same thing as Betty. Pepperoni? I hoped it wasn't hot. But when Betty ordered blue-cheese dressing for her salad, I drew the line. I would *not* eat blue cheese or anything made from cheese with blue on it, fancy restaurant or not. Blue cheese was moldy, rotten, something to throw away. Just forget the blue cheese.

Obviously sensing my reluctance, Betty asked, "Have you ever eaten blue-cheese dressing?" Laughingly, I admitted that I hadn't. "Well, then, just try it, and if you don't agree that it's absolutely delicious, put it aside and you can order something else."

As I agreed to her suggestion, I was thinking of the French dressing that would season my second salad. But I didn't think of the salad or the dressing for long. Something much more interesting had grabbed my attention.

Seated nearby at a round table were five or six young men. Even seated, they appeared larger than the young men I knew or the others who were in Gino's. Laughing loudly and speaking with northern accents, their heads were turned in our direction. The young Yankee giants were playing some kind of game that involved writing on a nap-kin or small piece of paper. It was, I quickly decided, a northern game.

My focus shifted from the young giants and their silly game to the salad that was placed before me. Cautiously, I took a small bite of the lettuce and blue-cheese dressing and waited for my sense of taste to render its verdict. Different, yes; rotten no!

Settling in to enjoy the salad, I was startled to hear our waitress, stand-ing by my side, say, "The young men at the round table sent this to you."

She handed me a piece of paper wound into a small square. Glancing over at the round table, I noticed, with a small amount of amusement and a large amount of curiosity, that the young giants were watching me.

"What is it?" Betty asked.

"Who knows? Do I ignore or open it?"

Without waiting for a response, I unwound the square paper. The words were simple and direct: "Who are you? Where do you live?" My response was to pass the note to Betty and continue eating.

By the time the pizza arrived, two of the very tall young men were sitting at our table, and our conversation was lively and long. That some of the other patrons glanced our way didn't intimidate me at all. If anyone were rude, I felt certain these young giants would keep us safe.

After two of the young northern giants had deposited us safely back at Vann dorm with a promise to call soon, I floated back to Room 209. Betty asked if I believed their story about being NC State basketball players. I said no. That really didn't matter to me, but my dad would think it interesting, if it were true. What mattered to me was that they were fun and attractive and seemed interested in us.

This Angel life was exactly what I'd hoped it would be. Yes, this Angel was ready to fly. I went to bed with a happy heart.

Terrible Turbulence

Monday came, and that meant classes and study time. The walkways and hallways were filled with upper-class students who had returned to the campus during the weekend. My clothes, a simple skirt and blouse, looked very similar to what the other students wore, so that was good. And even better, I got relatively few stares from students as I walked to my first class. I was not afraid of beginning college classes—just curious.

World history was taught by Dr. Alice Keith, a thin, soft-spoken, middle-aged woman with salt-and-pepper hair. After handing out what appeared to be a thick loose-leaf binder (which she called a syllabus) to each of us, Dr. Keith explained that all of our assignments for the year were contained in this binder. It included study guides, complete with questions that should be answered. The text and reference books were in the library. Our job was to go to the library, read, take notes, and remember all the important facts. Surely, that couldn't be too hard.

Algebra class was next, and I didn't look forward to it. But only one year was required, I reminded myself. Dr. Canady, a tall, broad-shouldered man with shaggy salt-and-pepper hair and thick-lensed glasses, was a commanding presence in the classroom. Standing at the chalkboard, he rushed through the class roll, gave us a little information about what to expect, and then began to talk and write numbers and symbols simultaneously. The scribbles (which I assumed were equations), the eraser (to remove them from the board), and his spoken words moved at the speed of lightning. This was an alien world, and I knew nothing. After receiving the next class assignment, I left feeling dazed.

English was my final class that day, and I was certain it wouldn't have the same terrible impact that algebra had produced. Miss Holland, my English instructor, could have been anywhere from age thirty-five to sixty. She, like the other professors I'd encountered, prefaced our last names with Miss when she took attendance. After a brief overview of the semester's work, she instructed us to write about something interesting we'd done over the summer.

As pencils began to record the memories of summer activities of the twenty to thirty freshman women in that sunlit classroom, I sat immobile. Nothing of any interest came to mind, not one thing. My summer was a repeat of summers past: putting in tobacco and helping Mama around the house. I thought and thought and looked around the room. My classmates were hard at work.

"What if nothing really interesting happened to you this past summer?" I blurted out.

Heads turned at the sound of my words, and Miss Holland looked at me quietly. There was no emotion on her face or in her voice as she replied, "Then, just write about something you did."

But what? And how? No interesting thoughts or words about summer were stored where I could retrieve them.

As I looked out the window, in the distance I saw a wooden fence and a huge span of pastureland full of barren, brown grass. There was nothing there to help me, and there was still nothing in my brain. My brain was as barren as the brown, dead grass outdoors.

With a growing sense of frustration and shame, I scribbled a few lines on a blank piece of composition paper and wrote my name, room number, and the date in the top-right-hand corner. I knew this was not acceptable work, and I felt far worse than terrible. But it was all I could do.

I heard and recorded the assignment for the next class. I left hoping that I wouldn't have a writing assignment of this kind again. But somehow, I knew that I would face this again; most likely it would be soon. My departure from my first college English class was marked by fear and dread.

Leaving Miss Holland's English class in emotional shambles, I returned to my room and did as much of the math and English assignments as I could, which wasn't much. I would get it in both classes the next time I went to them, I told myself. After dinner—though in my head it was still "supper"—I would head to the library and attend to the world-history homework that awaited me in that syllabus.

World history had never been of interest to me. So, already feeling bored, I trudged to the library that night and began the required reading. It didn't take long before my reading turned to skimming. I took few notes. Then, with very slow steps, I walked back to my room. My brain cells had shut down. I'd had enough surprises and anxiety for one day. Maybe the second day of college classes would be easier.

Though Latin was truly a foreign language, it didn't frighten me nearly as much as English and math. Mrs. Margaret Martin, the instructor, was a soft-spoken southern woman who said that we would learn vocabulary, grammar, and prefixes and suffixes that were found in many commonly used words. As she talked, I found myself interested and hopeful. I was very grateful to find hope anywhere, in any form.

The second class of the second day was a required religion class, the study of the Old Testament. Dr. Roger Crook's manner was mild and reminded me of my dad. Whatever he said didn't frighten me, nor did it excite me. But really, who had ever gotten excited about the Old Testament? I did wonder if we'd have to read every word of the Old Testament. The version of the Bible we'd had to buy for this class was huge. Randomly, I thought of the Ten Mile Center Baptist preachers and decided that Dr. Crook wouldn't shout out his beliefs, no matter what we were studying. That made me smile.

Later that day it was time for physical-education class. As thirty or forty of us gathered at one of the large playing fields behind the dining hall, I began to wonder what kind of physical education this would be. I saw no basketball courts, softball diamonds, or volleyball courts. What else could one play other than tennis? And why were we here when the tennis courts were in another location?

Soon, the instructor, Helena Allen, spoke: "Divide up into two teams and play until I blow the whistle."

Teams formed somehow, and soon we were all whooping and running. It seemed that the object was to kick a ball that was round and looked somewhat like a volleyball, except that it wasn't. Oh, keep the ball away from the other team. Somehow I'd missed the name of this game and the playing instructions. But the game went on. I ran with my team, hoping that I didn't do anything crazy that would call attention to the fact that I was lost in the middle of a large group that seemed to know exactly what was going on. Never did I confess that I knew nothing about the game.

Two days! That's exactly how long it took to discover that college classes were very different from what I had expected. Instead of an Angel flying gracefully and happily fluttering her wings from class to class, I had faltered. I was more like a fish out of water, with no one to throw me back into the pond. The fear I felt about my classes created terrible turbulence in my heart.

No Bumps Here

As terrible as my academic life was, my social life was terrific. The young giants Betty and I had met at Gino's did call, and it was a huge surprise to discover that they were, indeed, basketball players at NC State. The young men I'd met at a freshman mixer on campus also called. Oh, I loved this part of college life!

Each dorm floor had two telephones. One was on a desk that held a composition book and pencils; the other was a few steps away, in an actual telephone booth constructed of wood. Whoever was nearest the phone would answer it and yell the name of whoever was receiving the call. If the Angel were not there to take the call, then the message would be recorded in the composition book. At night, during study hours, a student answered the phone and recorded the names of the girls who received calls and recorded any messages.

Both phones rang constantly, and it seemed that at least half the calls were for either Jean Edwards or, oddly enough, Jayne Edwards. Jean was an all-American North Carolina beauty with long, straight, blond hair and a slim, feminine body, while Jayne was a Georgia belle with wavy, almost waist-length brown hair, bedroom eyes, and curves galore. They were the "queens of hoped-for dates" for many, many young men.

Though my name was not called as much as those of either of the Edwards girls, I received many more phone calls than I expected. I listened as the young men, none of whom I had known before arriving at Meredith, explained who they were, where they'd seen or met me, and how they'd gotten my name and phone number. With real interest, I listened to what their plans were for a date and then made a decision about whether I'd go out with them or not. Quite happily, my date calendar was usually booked far in advance of the weekend.

On a rare Friday night when I had no plans, Betty and I attended a mixer at the college union at NC State. There we were approached by a young man with dark, curly hair who was a student in the School of Design and his blond friend, who was a fourth-year landscape design student. Very quickly, I learned that the young man with dark, curly hair was from Lumberton. It was a moment of great surprise and genuine discomfort.

A white boy from Lumberton was being openly friendly? Was he interested in knowing me, or was his intent to ridicule my heritage? The fears of the past were now present. I could only pretend to be calm and talk as if this were an ordinary conversation. I hoped nothing racist or demeaning came from the lips of the Lumberton boy. And nothing did.

A few days later, the blond friend of the Lumberton boy called. From the bottom of my emotional storehouse where thoughts and feelings reside, old fears rose to the surface. What had the Lumberton boy said to Mr. Landscape Architecture about my people? About relations between whites and Indians? About Indian women? But I never asked and never found out. According to Mama and Grandmother Smith, there was no need to look for trouble.

Movies, dinners, dances, football games, and parties kept me busy and happy. I expected the second glances and hard stares, and they were obvious to me. But no one said anything (at least not that I heard), and I did what Mama said: "Smile and move on." *Maybe*, I thought, *these white boys will get accustomed to seeing a brown-skinned Meredith girl. I hope so. If not, I'll just follow Mama's advice.*

A few times, a date involved going to an event or location that was not on the "approved" list kept by Miss Louise Fleming, the dean of students. A date to the Duke Gardens in Durham with Mr. Landscape Architecture was one. I was out of town without permission. The risks that I took could have caused my immediate expulsion. And I knew that was serious business. But my reasoning was that if another Meredith student saw me where I didn't have permission to be, then she was guilty of the same offense and wouldn't report me.

It became apparent soon after I began dating at Meredith that my social life would not include fraternity members, as was true for many of my classmates. And that was fine. But I did wonder why. Was it my style, or lack of it, or my personality? Were they bound so closely together by the wealth or social status of their families that their dates had to come from similar groups? Or were fraternity members not allowed to bring nonwhite guests to their events?

I didn't spend much time analyzing that aspect of my new life. Neither my personal characteristics, anyone's social status, nor a white-only mentality were likely to change. What mattered most was that no bumps would mar my busy social life.

More Turbulence

As the days turned into weeks, neither my comfort level nor my performance improved in my classes. Algebra had gotten even worse than the first day I'd sat in Dr. Canady's class. After talking to Betty about the situation, I took the daring step of dropping algebra. Terrified, I made an appointment with my faculty adviser and, after providing a minimum of details, got the drop-slip signed. My parents had no idea what I'd done, and I knew I'd have some explaining to do. But for now, I rejoiced that college algebra was out of my life.

History and English were my personal demons. Rarely did I answer a question in history class that pleased Dr. Keith; she always had an added statement or question that delved deeper than what I knew. My pop quizzes and regular test grades were rarely above a D+. English was even more appalling. No matter what the assignment, my grades were barely above failing. The writing assignments were so heavily marked with red that I quit trying to decipher the little scribbles Miss Holland made on my papers.

It was the midterm physical-education exam that made it perfectly clear that I would not last a full year at Meredith. I was stunned to learn that we would have a written test on the rules of the strange game we had played for hours on end. Not surprisingly, my grade on that exam was a perfect F. As I left from that class with the failing exam papers in my hand, the tears began.

This Meredith Angel had faltered badly. In fact, this Meredith Angel was failing fast and furiously. With tears still falling, I found a secluded spot near the dining hall and sat down. There, among the shrubs, I sobbed.

As my crying subsided, random thoughts formed in my head. *How will I tell my parents I'm failing? What explanation can I give to the extended family and many friends who were so proud of me as I left Robeson County for Meredith?* And the thought that hurt the most was this: *If you fail, then you have failed your people.* This thought lingered for a long time. No one would ever say that to me, I knew, but I felt that being the first American Indian from our community to attend Meredith was a personal responsibility. Failing myself, my family, and my people would be more terrible than I could bear. The turbulence of my emotions threatened me like nothing I'd known.

In desperation, I bowed my head and prayed: "God, you know that I'm in trouble—big trouble. I can't fix this; I don't know how. I'm begging you to help me. Please help me. Amen."

With tears dried and a calm but heartbroken spirit, I walked, not to my room but to the playing fields, where I found my physical-education instructor. Timidly, I approached her and asked a single question: "Is it possible for me to pass this semester?"

Looking at me with a level gaze, she replied, "Only with a great deal of improvement in your test and participation grades. That's what it would take."

I thanked her and walked quickly and quietly to my room. Sitting on my bed, I reviewed my choices: give up and go home in disgrace or buckle down, study harder, and participate more in all my classes. I would hope and pray that, with my efforts and God's help, I wouldn't flunk out of college. Did I have a choice? Not in my mind. I hadn't come to Meredith to fail.

Hovering

My first visit home was shortly after our midterm grades were mailed to parents. This, I knew, was done on purpose. Those Meredith students who had done well would be welcomed home with rejoicing. My welcome would be different. I was the prodigal daughter, dreading what awaited me. My parents had received grades that were mostly Ds, only a matter of points from the F of failure. Only my C– in Latin was close to being respectable.

I was greeted by hellos, hugs, and smiles; I was surrounded by pure love, much laughter, and my favorite foods that short weekend. No one spoke a word about my poor academic status until it was almost time to leave.

"Lena," my mother said. "I know it's been a very hard time for you at Meredith. Your dad and I understand that it's a big adjustment for you to make the transition from Magnolia to Meredith. But we believe you can, and will, do it. Continue to study hard and have faith that God will help you."

Oh Lord, I thought as a knot of love, anxiety, and guilt lodged tightly in my throat. *Please don't talk about love and religion. I will absolutely fall apart. I do love you and Daddy for not making me feel like a failing jerk. But I'm so embarrassed and ashamed.* I had no voice nor words.

"Oh, I forgot to ask," Mama said after a minute. "How's your social life?"

Surprised by her sudden change of topics, I hesitated briefly before I lied: "I've met a few boys and gone out some," I said.

"Well, that's good," Mama said simply.

The solitude of the Trailways bus ride back to Raleigh gave me time to think about the terrible situation I faced. And without much effort or soul searching, I came to the following conclusions: I didn't read all of the assigned readings, nor did I answer all the study questions in world history. I didn't spend enough time learning the Latin vocabulary, and I put even less time into translations. And I found the game of soccer, or whatever its name was, boring. English? Well, that was an entirely different issue. Vocabulary was not the problem. I simply didn't know how to write. It was the formatting from beginning to ending that left me with a D– average.

So, here I was wanting to succeed and doing just the opposite. Had I glided through high school because the classes were so easy? Had I not received the preparation that other Meredith students had? Only God knew the answer. And it really didn't matter. What mattered was how I was going to change my failing grades to passing ones. And I remembered, rather guiltily, an admonition from my much-loved Aunt Lois: God helps those who help themselves.

Bumping Along

The second half of that first semester went by quickly. Despite my pleas to God and promises to myself, not much changed in the academic portion of this Angel's life. I went to classes and convinced myself that I was studying more and in better ways. The truth was that I was bumping along with no real improvements. I was barely passing any of my classes. My social life would have made the honor roll had there been one for dates and fun.

Meredith had no sororities, but I had heard about two societies whose purposes were never clear to me. I also didn't know of any differences between them. I believed that the emphasis was on which society had the most members. Having freshmen join one of the societies was a source of good-spirited competition among those who were members of the returning classes.

Shortly after joining the Astrotekton Society, I excitedly placed an order for a white wool blazer with the Meredith College symbol on its upper-front pocket. Thick gold trim identified the wearer as a member of the Astrotekton Society. My mother had strongly suggested that I wait to buy this expensive blazer, but my desire to have it was so great that I went against her wishes and ordered it anyway. I didn't think about the very real possibility of flunking out of Meredith. Nor did I consider that the blazer would have no use but to mock me if I were not a Meredith student. Denial of the facts about my academic status and thoughts of Christmas were equally strong in my dazed and dazzled brain.

Confrontations

It wasn't until I was back home in Saddletree for Christmas vacation that the realities of Robeson County resurfaced with a significant force. The daily reminders of the legal separation of white, Indian, and black people had been largely absent when I was in Raleigh. I was surrounded by white people there, and my interactions with them were not publicly challenged. But in Robeson County, whites, blacks, and Indians still lived, loved, and died in separate worlds.

One day, I went to Lumberton with my dad. Proudly wearing my Meredith Astrotekton blazer, we entered the Scottish Bank. While waiting in line to conduct business, Dad left to speak to someone nearby. As I turned to see who Dad was greeting, a well-dressed white man behind me stared hard in my direction and then said, "That's a nice-looking blazer you have."

"Thank you," I happily responded.

"How did you get it?"

"I ordered it," I replied, thinking that his question was very dumb.

After a brief pause, he looked at me with a steely gaze and said, "What I meant was, who gave it to you?"

I was stunned! And then I was angry, really angry. I knew exactly what he was thinking: Meredith is a college for white girls. And you, Indian girl, aren't white. So quit lying and tell the truth.

Barely able to breathe, I swallowed deeply. Speaking as clearly as I could and louder than normal, I said, "I am a student at Meredith College. That's how I got this blazer, and that's why I'm wearing it."

His eyes opened wide. He stared at me for a second or so, and he then turned slightly and stared at something in the distance. As he stood there, silent and shocked, I stood, too, feeling angry and proud. With a silent curse and an overwhelming desire to hurt him, I thought, *Your world is changing, Mr. White Man. And I'm helping change it. Get used to it.*

*C*hristmas vacation ended, and classes resumed. The exams loomed large. Reading days arrived, but one had to take an occasional break, and that meant a date. But I knew that my exam scores would be the deciding factor in whether I continued at Meredith or went back to Robeson County. I studied harder than ever and reviewed in every possible way I knew.

When my last exam was over, I had no idea whether I'd failed miserably or found a way to hang on. I could only wait, hope, and pray that my faltering beginning would evolve into a chance for this scared brown Angel to learn how to fly.

The air was thick with tension and anxiety as I waited for my semester grades to be computed, recorded, and placed in our mailboxes. While some professors posted grades outside their offices, I decided not to check those who did. Seeing an F on the way to another exam would have meant certain failure in another class. Waiting to receive the official report was harder than anything I'd ever done. That included the wait to be seated in the dentist's chair.

A peek into my post-office box showed the small envelope Betty had told me to expect. Pulling it out with trembling hands, I was aware of soft sighs around me. They were the sounds of other Angels who had opened their own private messages from heaven or hell.

It was not until I was out of the post office and away from everyone else that I stood, alone, and opened the envelope that would determine my future. My eyes quickly scanned the small printed card. Stunned, I exhaled. There wasn't an F on the card. In fact, there was only one D. I had *not* failed. Quickly, I thanked God and danced happily all the way back to share the good news with Betty. But she wasn't there.

Oh, I had faltered. Really, really faltered. I had almost failed. But I now had a second chance. The phrase rang over and over again in my head. A second chance. Second semester would be different. I didn't know how. But given a second chance, I would find a way to avoid faltering again.

Second-Chance Angel

*M*y second-semester classes were continuations of the subjects that had caused so much dismay and doubt during the first half of my freshman year. I kept my promises to God and myself as I listened and took many notes. I took more trips to the library to study world history, and I studied Latin vocabulary with increased intensity. English papers received a great deal of thought and many revisions. But neither my history nor English quizzes reflected grades above a D. I was back on the faltering fast track. Again, my hopes of success were rapidly disappearing.

Not long after I'd received dismal grades on two history quizzes, Dr. Keith requested that I meet with her immediately after class. Embarrassed and scared, I entered her office and was directed to sit in a chair next to her desk. She wasted no time in getting to the reason for my being in her office.

"Miss Epps," she began, "I know you're having trouble in my class. You're barely passing. You're intelligent enough to do the work. I know that. But you are *not* reading and completing the assignments as you should. If you'll do that, then your grades will be different—much different."

Unable to refute this, I nodded my head in agreement. "Why don't you read every word, take detailed notes, answer all of the study questions, and see if that doesn't make this class easier for you?" she asked.

I agreed that I would, thanked her insincerely, and left quickly. Stung by the truth, I knew that the "mystery" of my near-failing history grade was a secret no longer. Too much time on the telephone, too much time trying to learn how to play bridge, and too much time chatting about dates were costing me decent grades in history and my other classes.

I had no excuse for not getting better grades. I simply had to make academics a higher priority than my social life. That was the solution. It wasn't a change I wanted to make, but the second chance I'd been given was a last chance for Angel life. And I did want to remain a Meredith Angel.

With Dr. Keith's directives firmly implanted in my brain, I did as she suggested. The assignments were still boring, but I did them, and my participation in class discussions increased. Just as Dr. Keith predicted, my test grades were much better. English continued to be a stumbling block, and nothing I did improved my work or grades. In sheer desperation, I made an appointment with Miss Holland in March. Maybe, I hoped, she would be compassionate and helpful.

Miss Holland was quiet as I described my inability and frustration in being unable to write an essay that produced a passing grade. I was prepared for her to say that she was well aware of this and that it wasn't her problem. Instead, she proceeded to give me a short tutorial on how to construct an essay: the topic, a topic sentence for each paragraph, paragraphs that were in proper chronology, and an ending that was a summary of the previous paragraphs or main point.

She uttered no words of ridicule or made any disparaging remarks. She said she hoped our meeting would help. With a soft voice, she invited me to come back if I needed additional assistance. My thank-you was heartfelt, and, for the first time, I felt the beginnings of hope surge where English was concerned. Maybe I had the solution for an English paper that would produce a solid passing grade.

Success didn't come overnight, but each paper I turned in was returned with fewer red scribbles. I didn't get any As or Bs, but that didn't matter. I was producing acceptable work.

Academically, what interested me most was a surprise. The New Testament class that all Meredith Angels were required to take grabbed my attention early and never wavered. Dr. Crook, with his soft voice, small smile, and enormous knowledge of every aspect of the Bible, opened my mind to new ways of studying and interpreting the New Testament. He illuminated and expanded on what I'd been taught in a thoughtful and thought-provoking manner. Just as I'd believed! Just as I'd hoped!

In my worst "I told you so" voice, I shared some of what Dr. Crook had said, or what I thought he had said, with my mother. Ever wise, she never took the bait I offered to dispute my college professor or demean the religious instruction I'd received at our home church. She'd listen, ask questions, and encourage me to learn more.

Just as the bees began to buzz and the shrubs and flowers were full of fat buds, I, too, experienced the wonder of developing buds. They were buds of academic success. None of my papers or tests were marked with an F or D, and that included history and English.

One of the biggest surprises was that I still had an active social life. It was rare when I didn't date each night of the weekend, and often on Sunday afternoons and nights. Usually, each date was with a different young man, though I did date several of the same young men through-out my freshman year. There was no reason I could think of, except for big love, to limit myself to dating one person. Neither love nor limits were on my self-set horizon.

Coming as they did from tiny western mountain towns, small farms in the flatlands of "down east," and midsize towns of the piedmont of North Carolina, the young men I dated were interesting, well mannered, and fun. Some of them majored in forestry, design, and different kinds of engineering. Fraternity parties weren't part of my social scene, and that didn't matter. What mattered was that I was treated as the young

American Indian woman I envisioned myself to be. I didn't give any young men who didn't meet my criteria second chances.

My delight in having an active social life was not without moments of anxiousness and obnoxiousness. For much of both the first and second semesters of my first year at Meredith, I had moments when I experienced those stares I knew well and dreaded. The most usual places for this to occur on campus were in one of the parlors where I had gone to meet a date or on the breezeway where many couples said good night. With my head held high and a half smile on my lips, I focused on saying hello or good night and ignored, as much as possible, the eyes of those young men who looked at me with surprise or disdain.

It was when a date and I were at a public place—a theater, a restaurant, or a bar with music—when I felt most vulnerable. Would the manager allow us to enter? Would we be directed to seats reserved for colored people? What if we were seated inside and then asked to leave? Would someone in one of the venues point at us and make disparaging comments? Though this never happened, I was acutely aware of the possibility. It was a silent fear that lived in my head but affected my body. My heart always beat faster than usual until enough time had passed that I was reasonably certain that no one was going to make an issue of my presence. My relief at experiencing no verbal or physical insults was as real as the fun I had once my heartbeat slowed and I relaxed.

The spring of my freshman year at Meredith was picture perfect. Many of the trees scattered around the campus bloomed and added colorful beauty to the Angel Farm. The pasturelands that were visible from the English classroom and fields surrounding the entrance to the campus turned green. And once again, May Day came with all its glory.

Even more beautiful than all the flowering trees, shrubs, and the May court was the sight of solid, passing grades. Certainly, they weren't as good as I wanted them to be, but I was no longer a faltering Angel. I would not fail. I would not return to Saddletree in disgrace. And Mama was right: much of what I needed was to find the right balance between academic requirements and social activities.

At the end of my freshman year, I was stronger emotionally than when I had entered. And I had learned the hard way the secret to academic success as a Meredith girl. All this happened because of a second chance.

Get ready, sophomore year. I'm ready to spread my Angel wings.

Putting on Wings

*A*fter a Robeson County summer of helping put in tobacco, snapping green beans, being "little mama" to my brothers, and having few social activities, my desire to leave Saddletree was huge. I was eager to return for my sophomore year at Meredith.

It was a great relief to find that as difficult as my academic studies had been as a freshman, my sophomore year at Meredith seemed to be just the opposite. The courses were not easy, by any measure, but the challenges they presented were achievable.

I actually looked forward to attending the courses about local and federal government. My interest in this topic stemmed from what I'd heard and learned at home as we read the local newspaper, the *Robesonian*, and the Raleigh newspaper, the *News and Observer*, and watched the evening news on WRAL. What local and federal governments did or didn't do had relevance to my world. Preparing for and participating in these classes was not drudgery. I quickly decided that I would minor in government studies.

Biology and Dr. John Yarborough were a requirement. Learning about cells and other strange information about animals was useless, in my opinion, and dissecting anything was simply disgusting. Somehow, I managed to receive a respectable grade for the first semester.

It was in the second semester that some real barriers to success developed in biology. The barriers grew on trees. Dr. Yarborough instructed us to walk around campus and find trees with identification tags and to know those trees by the shape of their leaves. He even gave us papers with the shapes and names of the leaves to study.

Get to know leaves? Holly was not a stranger, and I recognized cedar as a common tree in Person County. Magnolias grew in some of the yards in Robeson County, and pine needles were abundant in our front yard. But I wasn't at all interested in trees or leaves, and my lab grades reflected that. I would have to study harder before exams. No leaf was going to keep me from being an Angel.

Though I did not love Latin, I found it interesting. Struggling to read Virgil's *Aeneid* was tedious and boring, but I enjoyed learning about the many words in the English language that have Latin prefixes, suffixes, and root words. This was practical information, and I knew it would be helpful in the future. That made studying worthwhile. Mrs. Martin was right: Latin is not an entirely dead language.

English was no longer a source of terror for me. With the help of Miss Holland firmly engrained in my brain, compositions lost their hostage hold on me. My joy at receiving grades no lower than a B– on five essays on Wordsworth's poetry was the highlight of the academic year. That others I knew received A grades meant little to me; I was happy for them. Miss Gorsage, the English instructor, likely had no idea why I smiled so broadly. But for me, those English essays with a grade of B signaled that I had earned my Angel wings. With deep gratitude and a few muted giggles, I rejoiced.

The first course that was part of the education major I had declared was educational psychology. Dr. David Revely, a tall, broad-shoulder man with a ruddy face, was head of the department and the instructor of this class. For the most part, the class was bland, with an occasional bit of dry humor injected by Dr. Revely.

At one point, we were learning about emotions and how they affect human beings. During one class, we discussed *hate*. Dr. Revely instructed each of us to name something we hated. I listened as my classmates said snakes, rutabagas, cancer, and a variety of other things. The sweet and lovely Jayne Edwards, sitting next to me, answered that she hated nothing.

"Miss Epps, what do you hate?" Dr. Revely asked.

Without a moment's hesitation, I replied, "I hate prejudice."

I hadn't planned to say that word. It just came out of my mouth by itself. As the word reverberated around the classroom, I looked at Dr. Revely. His face had a strained look on it, and tightly wound muscles showed on each jaw. *Oh Lord*, I thought. *That was a mistake—a big one. Why didn't I say scorpions?* But by then, the other students were naming what they hated, and Dr. Revely continued his lecture.

When the class was dismissed, I expected Dr. Revely to make a comment as I passed his desk. Or worse, I thought he might ask me to step into his office for a short conversation. But he did neither. Relieved, I left, but regret went with me. The honesty I expressed openly was a feeling I hadn't shared with anyone at Meredith. I wondered if it would make a difference in how Dr. Revely treated me and how my classmates felt about me. I hoped not.

Physical education was no longer an activity I'd never heard of. Horseback riding was what I took, and it almost killed me. One day, we were riding on a campus trail far away from the Meredith stables when a sudden thunderstorm erupted. My horse bolted and trotted as hard as she could toward the barn. The fact that I was as terrified of thunder and lightning as the horse was did nothing to help me control the animal or my nerves.

Barely hanging on, I managed to duck as we sped past low-hanging tree branches as thunder boomed all around us. As we entered the barn, the horse slowed as she found her stable. I sat on her back, drenched. The wetness could have been from rain drops, but I'm fairly certain it was from the sweat of fear. My grade for each semester was a B. Some said that everyone who took horseback riding received a B because extra tuition was required. But I'll always believe it was a gift from the instructor, who was extremely grateful I hadn't been hurt or gotten killed. The B certainly wasn't because of my equestrian skills.

*W*ith my academic Angel wings firmly attached, Meredith became a place where I was comfortable. Betty and I shared a single room at the northern end of first-floor Vann Hall. We also shared clothes, sometimes went out on double dates, visited each other's families, and enjoyed listening to all kinds of music on the stereo system I had brought from home. Sporadically, I would turn up the volume on my stereo system and open the door of our room. The bass sounds caused reverberations against the front door at the opposite end of the hall. It was time for an unplanned, unauthorized study break. Several girls would join Betty and me in the hall for an impromptu dance party.

That this happened in the middle of the required study hours resulted in a visit from the hall proctor. After receiving two or more warnings about noise and disruptions and learning that another one would result in some form of restriction or punishment, I put a quick and quiet end to that group activity. We closed our room door and dialed down the stereo volume to low. Party time in the hall was over.

Sometimes Betty and I spent a carefree afternoon in Cameron Village, usually after Saturday-morning classes. Cameron Village, reputed to be the first shopping center of its kind between Washington, DC and Atlanta, was a magical place. Department stores, specialty shops, restaurants, a shoe shop, and dry cleaners were all within walking distance of one another. The Kerr drugstore, with a long lunch counter decorated with NC State Wolfpack posters and memorabilia, was the perfect place to browse for small items or enjoy an afternoon snack.

Occasionally, we walked across the street to the S&W Cafeteria and had a meal that tasted more like Mama's cooking than any place I'd been in Raleigh. It was not uncommon to find a long line waiting to go through the cafeteria line. It was also not uncommon for many stares to be focused on Betty and me. Nervous as I was, I never suggested that we leave, nor did I mention the stares to Betty. We talked quietly about anything and everything as we inched our way toward the collards, corn, and cornbread that I enjoyed and reminded me of home. But always, I watched the stares of curious eyes and, sometimes, the hateful expressions on some of the faces.

After several visits there, Betty and I were standing in line when she mentioned that some of the people seemed to be watching us. "What's their problem?" she asked. "We just want to eat."

"Oh, they're just surprised to see us with our pale and dark skins together," I replied casually. *Let that be all*, I prayed silently.

On a later visit, the staring again greeted us, so Betty and I decided to give the staring people something to talk about. The two of us talked gibberish: absolutely made-up, unintelligible sounds, complete with inflections that sounded like a statement or question. And we did so loudly…and for a long time. That we weren't asked to leave because of the noise we made was a miracle. Surprisingly, the hard stares seemed to diminish.

After we sat down to eat our down-home meal, Betty and I collapsed in laughter.

"Well, those staring people have something to talk about now!" Betty said.

"Yes, they do," I agreed.

And I thought to myself, *I'll never forget how nervous this made me feel.* Oh Lord, what an experience!

Why or how I got the courage or nerve to engage in something that drew more attention than usual to my presence is something I can't explain. What this silliness accomplished, if anything, was likely nothing. The other customers probably wondered who we were and where we had come from. A white girl and that other one. Was she black, foreign, or what? That we did it meant that I had more self-confidence than ever. Or maybe I was more stupid and less sophisticated than I thought.

⟋⟍

With my academic life stabilized and my grades steadily improving, I had no qualms about dating, and I did so often. Some of the girls on my hall teased me and said that I had a "bag of snow," meaning that quite a few young men found me attractive. I dismissed the title "snow queen" as being silly and untrue, but I didn't deny that I loved having an active social life.

Most of the young men I dated were students at NC State and were upperclassmen. I thoroughly enjoyed the parties, dances, and football and basketball games. Not only was it fun to be part of the activities—though I knew absolutely nothing about football other than touchdowns—I loved dressing for the occasion. Good-looking suits for football games; sweater sets and matching skirts for basketball games, movies, and dinner; and stylish dresses with high-heeled shoes (preferably from Britain's) for parties, were the basics of being well dressed for dates.

Just as the grasses of the pastureland and lawn turned brown and were covered with leaves of bright gold, deep purple and the red of Winesap apples, I was assigned a research paper that required reference books from the NC State library. Betty and I visited the State library and returned to the Meredith campus with volumes on my assigned topic. Within an hour, I received a telephone call from someone I didn't know.

The young man explained that he and his friend saw me checking out books at the NC State library and made an agreement: whoever reached me first would not interfere with the other if I chose to date the first caller.

Amused and flattered, I listened as the young man told me that he was a junior studying aeronautical engineering and a member of a fraternity whose name I vaguely recognized. A fraternity man calling me?

That was unexpected. Definitely, this was a surprise. My amusement dimmed slightly. Would I go out with a fraternity man? Probably not! But he sounded nice, and if he or any of his fraternity brothers were rude or racist, I would handle it and return to campus. If he knew how to behave like a gentleman and I enjoyed being with him, then that would be fine. We made plans for the weekend.

Handsome, soft-spoken, and well mannered, this fraternity boy was a dream. His fraternity brothers were friendly and polite. The hostility I encountered came from a few of the fraternity brothers' dates. The girls' rudeness was for two reasons, I decided. They didn't expect to see a brown girl at the party, and they were envious that my date was Mr. Dreamboat. My reaction? I smiled sweetly and hoped they would see me often in the future.

Mr. Dreamboat and I dated many times in the coming months. In addition to believing that I was experiencing heaven on earth, I learned an important truth: not all fraternity boys are closed-minded racists, nor are they heirs to wealth and status.

But the best part of my social life was what I'd hoped and dreamed for: the young men accepted me as I was, a very young American Indian woman who liked to dress up, dance, talk, smoke cigarettes, sip an occasional alcoholic drink, and be treated with respect. It was the respect for my heritage that mattered most.

Some of the young men who dated Meredith girls still stared boldly when I was in their presence. I saw an occasional nudge in the ribs and head tossed in my direction. Nothing I could do would change their thoughts or behaviors. And really, that wasn't my job. I followed Mama's advice to stand tall and move on. What I continued to fear was that somewhere, off campus, a date and I would encounter hostile stares followed by hateful words, an invitation to leave, and a departure that left my date puzzled and me embarrassed and angry. But that didn't happen.

I didn't dwell on this possibility, but it was a constant companion as this brown American Indian girl lived, learned, and laughed in Raleigh. I was very glad to be a Meredith Angel, but I was always aware that I was a brown girl in a white-and-black world.

⤳

No matter what the Saturday afternoon or evening activities were, Meredith Angels were in church on Sunday morning for worship services. It hadn't taken many visits to several Baptist churches during my freshman year for Betty and me to decide that Pullen Memorial Baptist Church was where we'd attend. It was a large brick church with stained-glass windows, a balcony, an organ whose sound filled the sanctuary with classical music as well as more familiar hymns, and pews that were filled on Sundays at 11:00 a.m.

But it was none of those factors that caused me to attend Pullen faithfully. The Rev. Dr. W. W. Finlator was the pastor, and it was his messages that drew me to Pullen like a moth to light. Unlike the messages of temptation, damnation, and salvation of my childhood, Rev. Finlator seemed to assume that those of us present were believers in the Christian faith. His messages were often lights into my understanding of the Bible and their connection to present-day life.

From the pulpit, Rev. Finlator preached, cajoled, and challenged longtime members, students, and visitors to be people of peace and inclusion. He spoke about the failures of the French in Southeast Asia, and he spoke forcefully and directly about the horrors and wrongness of war as our country sent young men to Vietnam. He warned that increased involvement in this bloody struggle would create an awful divisiveness in our country.

The messages that touched me most deeply and dramatically were those that focused on the worth of *all* of God's children. *Judging and excluding anyone because of skin color was not only unfair*, Rev. Finlator said, *but biblically wrong*. He invited *all* people to worship at Pullen. He emphasized that worshipping with all of God's people was an important way to live the teachings of Christ rather than talk about them. He spoke of working for justice as a directive from God and loving others as a mandate from Jesus.

Amazed and energized with hope as I was, those messages from a white Baptist minister in Raleigh stirred a part of me that had been untouched by the pastors of my youth. Reflecting on those sermons, loaded with controversial ideas and theology, I sometimes thought that Rev. Finlator seemed oddly reminiscent of a biblical prophet. The newspaper reports indicated that many people were certain his words had no connection to God. But I was sure they were mistaken.

During the first week of February 1960, the *News and Observer* contained an account of what happened when four young black male college students staged a sit-in at the Woolworth's dime store lunch counter in Greensboro. Opposition to serving them was strong, and people feared violence. Hundreds of students, both black and white, arrived daily at the Woolworth's store in support of the sit-in; adults, both black and white, joined them. Across the state, the young men and their supporters received both encouragement and condemnation.

More than anything else, my reaction was genuine surprise. What these four young black students were doing was both shocking and brave. It was also extremely dangerous. That this event could have an impact on my life didn't cross my mind. On the Angel Farm, I heard no comments from students, faculty, or staff about the Woolworth's sit-in. Angel life continued as usual.

A few days later, Betty and I decided to go downtown. We did this, infrequently, to get away from our studies for a short while. After meandering in and out of a few stores, we headed to Woolworth's to have a snack. We'd been there before.

As we approached the entrance to Woolworth's, I noticed two very large white men standing on either side of the door. They said nothing as we got closer to them, but stared—hard. As their stares seem to pierce my body, Betty and I walked past them and took seats at the uncrowded lunch counter. We waited, but no one came to take our order. A couple of employees stood behind the counter, about six feet away, and looked in our direction occasionally.

"What's taking them so long to take our order?" Betty asked. "Let's move and sit at one of the little tables," she suggested. "Maybe they'll come there and take our order."

As we walked to a table, the images of the sit-in taking place in Greensboro appeared in my head. *These people don't know whether I'm black or Indian or what*, I thought. *Will they refuse to serve us? Will they call those two big white men who look like bouncers at a nightclub to escort us out of Woolworth's?* My heart beat louder and quicker as I willed myself to remain calm.

While the few customers in the lunch area of the store watched, a waitress came over, gave us a thorough look, took our order, and returned with it quickly. My need for a Pepsi and some Nabs had diminished. I forced myself to take a few sips of Pepsi and eat a cracker. Then, I told Betty I was ready to leave.

The big bouncer-looking men glared without speaking as we left the store and headed for the nearest bus stop.

As Betty and I waited for the bus, I thought about the episode in Woolworth's and experienced great relief that we hadn't been told to leave. I was certain I knew exactly what explained the delay in our order being taken. "Betty," I began, "the guards at the door of Woolworth's were there to keep black people from coming inside or to take them out if they tried to sit at the counter and order food."

"And what does that have to do with us?" she asked.

Oh hell, here we go. It's time for the truth. Just say it and get it done, I thought. "The two guards thought I was black, and they were waiting to see what the waitresses would do. If they refused to serve us, then the guards would've asked us to leave," I said.

Betty looked at me for a long moment and replied, "Well, that's just stupid. Really stupid. You are Indian." There was a short moment of quiet before she spoke again. "Well, I'm glad nothing happened."

"Glad" was an understatement from my perspective. "Me too," I said.

Within a week, sit-ins were taking place in downtown Raleigh, and I made no plans to go to any of them or be near them. Why would anyone want to get involved in a black/white issue? I knew that some people might identify me as black. But I wasn't. People needed to learn the difference. The connection between what was taking place and my desire to be accepted as an Indian with brown skin didn't register with me. Rev. Finlator's Sunday messages that *all* Christians should work for justice were buried somewhere and didn't surface.

Our college administrators or professors didn't issue any calls to join in and support the Raleigh sit-ins (at least not that I heard of), and no student I talked to ever mentioned what was going on. Getting caught in the middle of what could be trouble was to be avoided, I'd always been taught. I was a brown Angel, unaware that the sit-ins could and would affect my life in the future.

As spring arrived and the campus changed from barren and brown to blooms of beauty, I sat in the same English classroom and remembered how lost and adrift I'd felt just a year earlier. This year had evolved into a beautiful one, long before spring arrived. My academic life was solid, and my social life was flourishing. Even my spiritual life had grown. As exams ended, instead of fear, I awaited my semester grades with anticipation, in spite of some serious trouble with leaves in Dr. Yarborough's biology class.

Sophomore year at Meredith in a word? Successful, in every way. Life was easier and better with Angel wings securely attached to my earthly body.

Flying High

I spent much of the summer before my junior year of college taking American history at Pembroke State College. In a classroom in the Old Main Building, Dean Clifton Oxendine, with few notes and much knowledge, took us from the beginning days to the present time of our country. When I provided the wrong name of a Southern general in the Civil War, Dean Oxendine chastised me gently by saying, "Your dad would be horrified; he was a history scholar."

We both smiled. And I smiled even more when I received an A in that class.

It was exciting to be returning to Meredith for my junior year. I felt no anxiety or concern about my ability to do the academic work successfully, and I'd almost completed the general college requirements of the curriculum. This year I would begin concentrating on courses that related to my major of elementary education and one of my minors, history. I looked forward to both.

Several other things excited me about being a junior Angel. My dear roommate, Betty Orr, had graduated in the spring, and I knew that I'd miss her. But she had a new life, and I'd have a new roommate and a new residence on the opposite side of the quadrangle. Janet Puckett (a mathematical genius from Richmond) and I would share a room and be suite mates of Yvonne Summey from Gastonia and Cindy Corbett from Tabor City, both small towns in North Carolina.

Janet and I were opposites in many ways. She had fair skin, eyes that sparkled when she laughed, and hair that seemed to curl without any rollers. Janet was extremely quiet, took her studies very seriously, and didn't socialize much. But she was good-natured, thoughtful, and had a dry wit that I liked. Her focus on academics and the future could only be a positive influence on me. We'd balance each other perfectly, I believed.

Second, I would officially become a "big sister" to sweet, fun-loving, pretty Teresa Covington, a freshman from Rockingham. We had corresponded throughout the summer and had met prior to the opening of the fall semester. Our personalities clicked immediately, and our hearts bonded instantly. Our sisterhood transcended our skin-color differences and revealed two young women who liked "boys" (our description of male college students), the beach, music, and mixed drinks. She was just the kind of sister I'd always wanted.

The third event that I looked forward to was receiving and wearing my Meredith College ring. The long oval onyx, with the Meredith "Lux" seal imprinted on it and encircled with white gold, was a sign of accomplishment. The underside of the white-gold ring would have my initials and 1962 engraved on it. The Meredith ring would be a visible symbol that I was on track to graduate from Meredith College. This brown Angel would proudly wear her Meredith ring, and yes, I would wave my ring hand often, especially when I returned home to visit my family. Surely, questions would be asked, and I would respond proudly.

Long before our class rings arrived, I was happily involved in my classes. My study habits were strong and consistent, and my midterm exams produced very good grades. The thought occurred to me that it was possible I might make the academic honor roll for first semester. What a thrill that would be! My parents would be overjoyed.

No waiting for the end of the semester was necessary to give myself an A in social life. From the day I arrived back for my junior year till the end of year, I was busy. From the usual movies, dinner dates, dances, and athletic events to private parties in apartments that were totally off-limits for us Angels, I enjoyed it all. Fortunately, no one reported me for being part of those fun but forbidden gatherings.

Flashing my Meredith ring at home was my favorite Christmas gift. This Angel was flying. But a few weeks later, I was soaring. This brown Meredith Angel had made the honor roll!

While second-semester classes focused on my education-major requirements, the class I enjoyed most was southern history. The class had about ten students, and Dr. Lemmon kept us busy reading a text and reference books, answering her complex questions in class, and taking pages of class notes. In the midst of one note-taking session, the lead in my pencil broke. As soon as it was polite to do so, I spoke. "Dr. Lemmon, do you have a pencil I may borrow? My lead broke."

"What did you say?" she asked.

"I need to borrow a pencil," I replied.

Sitting very erect and looking straight at me, she said, "Say what you need, again."

Feeling puzzled, I repeated my request. "A pencil. I need a pencil, please."

"That's not the way you pronounce the word. It's *pen*-cil, not pencil. Now say the word correctly.

Completely embarrassed, I said the word "pencil," and again she corrected me.

"You are pronouncing the *e* in the first syllable as a short *i*, not as a short *e*. You need to correct your speech. I expect proper English to be spoken." Finally, she handed me a pencil.

With a hot face and embarrassment oozing and engulfing me, I kept my eyes on the history notebook on my desk. I tried very hard to take notes, but my brain seemed muddled. Feeling completely humiliated, I walked quickly as I left the class. I hoped to avoid any conversation about the Dr. Lemmon dialogue with my classmates. They'd probably try to make some sort of little joke about it and tell me not to worry about it. But to me it was no joking matter.

I knew that my dialect was heavy southern. People often asked if I were from South Carolina, and I'd laugh and tell them that Saddletree was indeed near the South Carolina state line. But Dr. Lemmon's lecture was not really about a dialect. It was about formal usage of phonics and pronunciation. I recognized that and acknowledged that she was probably correct.

But I had spoken the same way ever since I'd arrived at Meredith. No faculty member or staff person had ever corrected my pronunciation of any word, with or without a short *e* in it. So why would she point out my error? And most especially, why would she do so in the presence of others? Would she do the same to a white student? I didn't think so. Whether it was correct or not, I believed that her regard for me as a brown-skinned student was less than what she had for her white students. At least at that time.

Though surprised and distressed, I decided that this unexpected, embarrassing lecture on speech wouldn't cause me to miss class, nor would it affect my grade. I would bring two sharpened pencils to class. But I was glad this was my last class with Dr. Lemmon.

The highlight of the year was the Junior Dance, a first at Meredith. When a request went out for parents to serve as chaperones, I quickly volunteered my parents. Though I knew my dad didn't dance and wasn't fond of social gatherings, I relied on my mother's love of social interaction to convince him that this was a wonderful opportunity to get a glimpse of my college activities. Mama and I were both delighted when Daddy agreed.

The night of the dance was extremely cold, and the ground was covered in frozen snow. Wearing a borrowed backless dress in bright-coral brocade fabric, stiletto heels, and white fake-fur jacket and having a handsome, blond date who drove a white TR-3, I was an angel in heaven on earth. That I slipped and fell just as I was trying to get into the white chariot of my Prince Charming didn't subdue my joy.

When Prince Charming and I approached the entrance of the stately Carolina Country Club, the black doorman cast stern eyes in my direction, but he said nothing as we walked through the door he opened and held for us. As we glided into the ballroom, music greeted us. *Let the music continue*, I thought. *This brown Meredith Angel has come to dance.* And Prince Charming and I did just that.

My father and mother watched from the sidelines. Daddy looked handsome and distinguished in a brown suit and beige shirt with French cuffs sporting elegant silver cufflinks. "Gracie," the name of endearment I sometimes called my mother, was never lovelier than that night. Her slim body was wrapped in a dress of pale tan silk with long roses that seemed to grow from the hem to her tiny waist. Yes, this was the dress that Mama said had caused her to have a headache when she'd bought it a year earlier, when she was in Texas for an educational conference. The dress was on sale at Neiman-Marcus, and Mama said she'd never tell my dad how much it cost. *Clearly, the dress was worth the cost*, I thought.

The Junior Dance was a heavenly affair. After all, it was for Angels, Meredith College Angels. And I was one of them.

⌒

Later in the spring, as a formal dance date with Mr. Dreamboat approached, I decided that I wanted short hair. More fashionable, maybe with bangs. Could I emulate a version of the Audrey Hepburn look? Or maybe the stylist would have some other suggestion. When I shared my plans with my little sister, Teresa, she suggested that we both make appointments. That way we could have some fun together.

The beauty salon was located in the Ridgewood Shopping Center, a short walk behind the Meredith campus. Tee and I entered the reception area, gave our names to the receptionist, and then laughed and talked as we found seats. As they peered from behind the covers of magazines, I was aware of people watching us. But that didn't surprise me. After all, I had plenty of experience with people watching my interactions with white people.

Very soon, stylists called for both Tee and me. As I walked a step or two in the direction of the stylist who'd called my name, she fired a verbal rocket that exploded violently in my ears.

"I don't do nigger hair."

It was loud, plain, and hit my core. Immobilized, I said nothing. I stood frozen, like a zombie. From beside me, or maybe it was far away, I heard a voice speaking. Was it Teresa who said, "What's wrong with you? What in the world are you talking about?"

With eyes flat, dull, and looking straight at me, the loud voice again proclaimed:

"I don't do nigger hair."

Still frozen, I stood, unable to move or speak. I never felt my heart beating. The voice I heard next spoke clearly and strongly. It was Teresa who said, "This is my Big Sister, Lena. And you are wrong. My sister is an American Indian, and don't you ever forget it." Pausing for a second, she continued, "Now, are you going to cut her hair, or is somebody else going to do it?"

The room was quiet, entirely silent. It was the silence that follows disbelief, distress, and destruction. It was attempted murder of my spirit. And it almost worked.

"I'll cut her hair," another voice nearby said.

With the motion of a robot, I moved toward the chair where that stylist stood. I'm sure we must have talked some, but I don't remember a word that was spoken. The rage, humiliation, and pain I felt left me feeling lifeless.

After my styling session ended and I paid the stylist, I found a chair, picked up a magazine, and waited for Teresa's session to end. After flipping through the magazine and being unable to read or even look at the photographs, I laid it down. I cried silent tears that didn't fall. I shouted angry words with an unheard voice. I burned hot with anger and shame and never broke a sweat. My heart beat wildly as I sat perfectly still.

It was then when I remembered what Mama had said: Some people won't like you because of your skin color. That is ignorant, and we both know it. *Just ignore those people and move on.*

Move on? I could barely sit up. But when Teresa was done, she and I walked out of that salon and never looked back. Somewhere along the way back to Meredith, Teresa expressed her outrage over what I'd experienced and vowed never to return there again.

"She was crazy, Lena, just plain crazy," Tee said with a voice full of dismay.

Crazy? I wasn't too sure about that. But I knew she was *ignorant* and that if I dwelled on her words and actions, my heart would hurt more than it did now. An *ignorant* hairdresser would *not* ruin my life, not on this spring day or any other day. I would move on and be glad that I could count on family and friends like Tee to stick up for me and, no matter what, stick with me.

⟵⟶

The negative experience of getting a new hairstyle faded as I heard positive comments about my new look. Sophisticated! Becoming! I liked those descriptions. Move on? Of course I did. But there were quiet moments when the humiliation and pain of being singled out for public discrimination returned. They were vivid reminders that just because I was a Meredith Angel in Raleigh, the issues of skin color and race as sources of hate and hurt had not disappeared. A brown Angel could be in heaven on earth on campus, but a few steps away, hell waited.

As the green of spring spread over the Angel Farm and flowers and trees created a blooming fairyland, I walked lightly with my head and its new hairstyle held high and proud. Telephone calls brought invitations for spring dates that were more special than those in the past, and my grades were solid, though not quite high enough for honor-roll status. With a Meredith ring on my finger, a smile on my face, and feet that barely touched the ground, my heart and soul overflowed with happiness.

This brown Angel was flying high!

Fight and Flight

Senior year! The very sound of it thrilled me. My class schedule was the least demanding of any I'd had at Meredith for two reasons. I had attended summer school—once again, at Pembroke State—and I'd completed the last of Meredith's required core classes, six hours of science. I looked forward to my classes and student teaching in the spring. Social life! Oh yes, lots of it, I told myself. And if my dad bought a car for me, I'd have unlimited freedom—within the boundaries of Meredith's rules, of course. Graduation would come, and this brown Angel would fly into a future full of opportunities to be my own person. But much of the reality was quite different. And the difference began with my social life.

For the first time since I'd been at Meredith, I didn't receive many telephone calls from young men asking for dates. As the days and weekends passed with very little social activity, I noticed that for many of my senior classmates, the opposite was true. They were busy every weekend and many weeknights as well. In fact, quite a few Meredith Angels were making plans for June weddings.

By October, I was certain I knew why my social life was virtually nonexistent. Most of the young men I'd dated were older and upperclassmen. They had either graduated or had made long-term commitments to other young women. I had never relied on much assistance from Meredith friends to fix me up with dates, and I wouldn't ask anyone to do that now. Dating younger men was not an option, in my book.

Senior year without a busy social life was different. I missed having dates…a great deal. But I knew with absolute certainty that I didn't want to be engaged or married anytime soon. I knew that I had to accept that senior year would have many lonely weekends and a fair amount of envy for those who dated often. Two hopes arose: that success would come in other areas and that my final year at Meredith would pass quickly.

⟵⟶

*A*cademically, everything went smoothly until mid-October. It was then when Dr. Revely, the head of the education department, asked me to drop by his office for a little talk. Greatly puzzled because my grades were good, I went to his office with no fear. Still, this entire thing seemed a bit mysterious.

"Hello and come in, Miss Epps," was Dr. Revely's welcome. "I suppose you're getting excited about student teaching in second semester."

"Oh yes, I'm looking forward to it," I replied.

"Miss Epps," he asked in a soft voice, "how would like to do your student teaching in Robeson County?"

Stunned by his question, I sat rigidly as total disbelief and deep anger engulfed every pore of my body. Outraged, I sat in a folding chair beside his desk and said nothing for a few seconds. Then I looked him straight in the eye and responded in a steely voice that I barely recognized as my own: "*Absolutely not*. I will *not* do student teaching in Robeson County. I came to Meredith for my education, and Meredith students don't do their student teaching in Robeson County. They are assigned to schools in the city of Raleigh public schools or are assigned to Wake County schools. That's where I intend to do my student teaching."

Dr. Revely continued to look at me with eyes that betrayed no emotion, and he spoke in that quiet voice of his I knew well. "Miss Epps, we have a problem. The city of Raleigh schools won't agree to your being a student teacher in their system. They will not assign you to a white school, and they think it unwise for you to be assigned to a black school. That's the situation. So, I thought…"

As his voice slowly trailed off into nothingness, I knew what he thought and hated every piece of it. All the pent-up anxiety and fear I'd ever felt since I came to Meredith gathered into a mixture of anger, disgust, and courage that exploded as I said in a hard-toned voice, "Dr. Revely, that is *not my problem*. This is *your problem*, and I expect you to solve it. Make sure that you understand: *I will not student teach in Robeson County*. My parents have paid a lot of money for me to attend Meredith, and they expect that I will be treated just the same as other Meredith students. I expect that, too. I don't know how you'll solve your problem, and I really don't care. But no, I will not do my student teaching in Robeson County."

Then, I stood up and walked out of his office. I was in shock. My legs felt weak as I walked the short distance to the quadrangle and lowered my body onto a bench. But it was my heart that worried me; it felt frozen even as it beat rapidly. Trying to sort out the different angles of this situation set off all the emotions I'd felt just a few minutes earlier. Anger, disbelief, dismay, more anger, and, finally, fear. Cold, hard fear.

What if I'd come this far and couldn't graduate from Meredith? After all the tears and frustrations and then all the accomplishments and fun, would I be denied a diploma because I couldn't be a student teacher in Raleigh or Wake County? Would my brown Indian skin keep me from graduating? *Oh God, this isn't fair*, I thought. *This is crazy. It's stupid*. When would this damn discrimination end?

As I sat motionless on that concrete bench, I realized that this was the only time since I'd been at Meredith that my mother's advice to "move on" seemed inadequate. I couldn't move on unless someone else moved first, moved fast, and did so with authority. It appeared that I had two choices: hope and pray that Dr. Revely would work this out, or call my dad and ask him to intervene. Dad would likely call Dr. Carlyle Campbell, the president of the college, and who knew what that call might create. More talks, more anguish, and more anxiety for me was a given. With absolute certainty, I knew my dad would find a way to solve this problem. But the truth was, I didn't want him to have to be involved. Let Meredith solve it. I was a Meredith Angel. It was Meredith College's responsibility to ensure that I taught in the same location as their other student teachers.

Gathering strength and resolve from somewhere deep inside that had previously been untapped, I made my way back to the room Janet and I shared. When she asked what the meeting with Dr. Revely had been about, I sighed and said, "Oh, just a few details about student teaching," as I flopped onto my bed.

As I pretended to read an assignment, my mind replayed the conversation with Dr. Revely until it could do so no more. It was then when I knew I had only one choice: keep up the good grades and pray that someone, somehow, would find a place for an Indian Angel to do student teaching.

⁓

One more time, Mama was right. *I had to move on.* And so I did. My classes went well, and I especially enjoyed those that dealt with political science. Sometimes, I listened as seniors who were doing their student teaching shared interesting and funny stories about their experiences. I hoped that I'd get to have that same experience, but I shared that burden with no one. Complaining or crying wouldn't change or help the situation. My job was to keep moving on.

Infrequently, I had dates in Raleigh or in Robeson County when I was at home for the weekend. Al Prevatte, a young white man from

Lumberton who worked in Raleigh, and Ruth Dial Roberts, an Indian woman from Pembroke who was a married Meredith day student and lived off campus, both had cars and were kind enough to give me rides to Saddletree and then back to Raleigh. It was a welcome change from riding the Trailways bus.

Thanksgiving was celebrated as usual with my family, who praised me for what I thought my semester grades would be. But it was difficult for me to answer the question about how I felt about student teaching in the spring semester.

"Oh, I'm sure it'll be fine," I lied.

Smile, I told myself, *and don't let Mama or Daddy hear or see your fear. Change the subject. Do what Mama said. Move on.*

The cold days of December arrived, and still there was no word about arrangements for my student teaching. A request to meet with Dr. Revely came several days before Christmas break, and our meeting was short and to the point. Cary Elementary School, part of the Wake County Public Schools system, had agreed for me to do student teaching. Several other Meredith girls would also be assigned to schools in Cary. My thank-you was brief, and my departure was quick. The relief I felt hit me as I walked from Joyner Hall into the open spaces of the campus. I could breathe and smile naturally again.

Christmas brought family, fun, and a white '62 Ford Falcon. It wasn't the sports car I wanted, but it was brand new and it was mine, paid in full by my dad. As I said my goodbyes when Christmas break ended, Daddy concluded with these words: "Lena, don't drive on Highway 50 between Benson and Garner. Go back the I-95 way."

"Why?" I asked.

"It isn't safe."

That seemed odd to me. Route 50 out of Benson was a paved two-lane road with more curves and twists than those in Robeson County, but other than that, it was much like the roads in Robeson County. Tobacco and cotton fields, shacks, houses, tobacco barns, and country stores dotted the landscape. But I promised I wouldn't travel that way and headed for Raleigh on I-95.

Exam week came and went, and my name was on the honor roll. I was one semester away from being a Meredith graduate. Nothing could stop me now. My flight to adult freedom would be smooth for the remainder of the time I was a brown Angel. No fights on this final part of my flight to freedom!

⌒

The final classes I took were interesting, and I prepared well for them. Most weekends were lonely and long, so sometimes I'd get in my white Falcon and head home to Saddletree. Love and laughter were always waiting for me there. It was after one of those weekends when I decided to take the shortcut back to the Angel Farm and leave I-95 at Benson and drive to Raleigh via the route my dad had warned me not to take.

As I was paying attention to the highway and its shoulders, a strange sight came into view ahead. A small group of people was walking on the shoulder of the road dressed in weird clothes. They all wore long white robes and tall, pointy hats. *What in the world is this?* I wondered. Slowing down as I passed them, I stared as I tried to figure out where they were going dressed like that on a late-Sunday afternoon in the middle of February.

As usual, I called my parents to let them know I was safely back at Meredith and then proceeded to tell my dad about the strange sight I'd seen on Highway 50. After a pause, he spoke. "Lena, what you saw were members of the Ku Klux Klan. Who knows where they were going or why. But that's the reason I told you to never travel on Highway 50. What if you'd had a flat tire or other car trouble? Who knows what might have happened to you?"

Stunned into silence and terrified at the thought of what might have happened, I could only mumble that *I would never, ever travel on Highway*

50 again. Daddy didn't ask me to make a promise to him. I made one to myself.

Soon, I was student teaching at Cary Elementary School. My supervising teacher, the students, and the staff there were respectful, supportive, and fun. My experience was very positive, and it wasn't long before I was thinking about getting a teaching job. I talked often with my suite mates, Yvonne Summey, a gifted artist who planned to teach, and Cindy Corbett, a star in the field of science, about where we'd live and work after we graduated. We decided that Winston-Salem would be the perfect place. It was a midsize city situated near the center of the state. Each of us could get home for a weekend with no difficulty, and, surely, Winston-Salem would offer plenty of social life because of the graduate and professional schools at Wake Forest University, in addition to the large number of corporate offices of businesses and industries there. Of course, Yvonne didn't care about the social life, as she was engaged, and Janet, my roommate, had a high-paying job waiting for her in the Norfolk, Virginia, area.

It was March when recruiters from the Winston-Salem school system came to our campus, and I had a very positive interview. My interviewer said he believed that I would enjoy living and working in Winston-Salem and that he would recommend to the school board that I be hired. Elated that I would receive a contract in a couple of weeks, I floated back to the dormitory.

Excitement filled the suite as Yvonne, Cindy, and I talked about the future in Winston-Salem. Janet promised that she would visit.

Easter came late in April of 1962, and I went home for the weekend full of excitement about being offered a job. For some reason, I decided to wait and share the good news on Sunday at our Easter dinner. Around ten on Saturday morning, my parents' phone rang, and I answered it. I was surprised to hear a man ask to speak to me. The caller was the recruiter from the Winston-Salem schools, and his message was this: the board of education had reviewed my application and, with regret, had rescinded the offer for me to teach in their school system.

"The problem, Miss Epps," the recruiter told me, "is that the board feels strongly that the white community will not accept you, and they will not assign you to a black school."

His words knocked all the words I knew out of me. I sat still, said nothing, and held onto the telephone. I hoped that I betrayed none of the shock, hurt, and hopelessness I felt to my parents, who were in the same room.

"Miss Epps, I am so terribly sorry," the recruiter said. "If I could do anything to change this, I would, but I can't. But I do have a message for you from the superintendent of schools, Dr. Clyde Phillips. He wants you to know that he deeply regrets that the board took this action. He also wants you to know that he will become superintendent of the Charlotte-Mecklenburg school system in early June and would love to have you as a teacher there. He urges you to submit an application to that system as soon as possible."

The entire conversation took only a few minutes, and I had not spoken. After a long pause, the recruiter again apologized for having to make this call and reiterated the superintendent's invitation. In a quiet voice, I told the man on the phone that I understood what he was saying, and I asked him to thank the superintendent for me.

"Goodbye," I said, and I hung up the phone.

Dumbfounded and dazed, I sat in my dad's tall Windsor telephone chair for what seemed like days. Not again! Oh yes, again! I felt no anger or outrage. I felt whipped, defeated, and just worn out by this senior year's second round of exclusion because of my American Indian heritage. What now? *I don't know, I simply don't know. But Easter will not be ruined. I'll smile and worry about this later.*

My thoughts were interrupted by Mama's cheerful voice. "Lena, who called?" she asked.

"Oh, it was a man calling about some jobs," I replied.

Mama and Daddy continued whatever they'd been doing, and I poured a large cup of coffee. After loading it with sugar, I sat thinking for a long time. A smile that I hoped didn't look too forced appeared on my face as I turned my attention to Mama and Daddy, my rambunctious brothers, Sunday church, and preparations for Easter dinner. The thoughts of the Easter baskets that were still placed next to our breakfast plates on Easter morning were not as exciting as in years past.

It was difficult for me to leave home that Easter Sunday afternoon. No doubt I realized that the safety and security I knew there would remain with my parents and the employment/race dilemma waited for me in Raleigh. Whatever the solution would be would have to come from me. The drive back to Meredith focused my thoughts on what to do next.

Not long after Easter, I told Janet and my suite mates that I'd changed my mind about moving to Winston-Salem. In a manner of casual nonchalance, I mentioned that Charlotte was a bigger city and would be an easier drive home for me, and the teacher salaries there were the highest in the state. No one raised any objections or questions. I mailed a letter and application for employment the next day.

In the midst of finishing classes, student teaching, and preparing for graduation, I started having nightmares. Actually, it was always the same nightmare. It was the day before graduation, and Dean Peacock called me into his office and told me that I wouldn't be able to graduate because I lacked one hour of course credit. Always, I pleaded and cried that I must graduate. Always, he said it wasn't possible. Always, I woke up terrified and in tears.

I checked my course credits by the year and, as I knew, I had the required number of credit hours plus three. My grade point average was fine, despite my faltering freshman year. Not once or twice did I recheck my academic standing, but several times. That didn't eliminate the dream that haunted many of my final nights on the Angel Farm.

The month of May brought a number of special events. The May Day celebration was as beautiful as ever. The class of 1962 May queen, Gwen Cooper, was lovely, and her attendants and their escorts added beauty and attractiveness to the treasured tradition on the quadrangle. A formal afternoon tea for seniors only was hosted by President Campbell in the parlors of Johnson Hall. Wearing our prettiest spring dresses and brightest smiles, we greeted President Campbell, the academic faculty, and administrative staff. I was taken aback when one male faculty member, whose classes I'd never attended, simply said, "Congratulations to one of the prettiest girls on campus." Totally surprised, I wondered why he would say that. There were dozens of pretty girls on campus. And not one of them was named Lena. Still, I was flattered.

Soon, the traditional white graduation dress was purchased and hung in my closet. Invitations to graduation ceremonies were addressed and mailed. I went to the graduation practices, listened to the laughter and excitement of my classmates, and enjoyed the status of being a graduating senior, except when I thought about the "not graduating" dream. I was excited that Betty Orr would see me *walk*.

Meanwhile in Robeson County, my mother found the perfect outfits for herself, my brothers, and Grandmother Lela. She made plans for an after-graduation picnic at Pullen Park, and she forced my young brothers to review good manners with her. Daddy did what he did best in such situations: he sat quietly, smiled occasionally, and waited for the Big Event.

Graduation weekend arrived as quickly as a Robeson County thunderstorm in summer. Graduation day was beautiful, with warm sunshine and glistening trees. Filing into Jones Hall, I looked at the auditorium filled with proud family members and friends and knew that mine were among them. I knew they were happy and pleased.

As my name was called and I accepted my diploma, I smiled and nodded my head slightly as Dean Peacock offered his congratulations. I had done it. I was a Meredith Angel forever and ever. No one could take this away from me. Ever. I was a brown Angel, and I was free to fly.

～⟋

*S*till with a big grin on my face, I stood on the steps of Jones Hall waiting for my parents to find me in the crowd of exuberant Angels and beaming families. I heard a familiar voice calling my name. "Lena, congratulations," the voice said.

Turning to the sound of the voice, I saw Rev. Finlator, who came toward me with a huge smile and stood very close as he spoke. "I'm so proud of you. And I know that you'll do great things in the future. May God bless you always."

With those words, he offered his hand, and I leaned toward him. Instead of taking his hand, though, I wrapped my arms around him in a hug. Big tears rolled down my face, and I made no effort to hide or wipe them away. After a few seconds, I whispered my thanks and moved to where I thought I'd be able to see my parents when they came outside.

As I waited for them to appear, I thought about Rev. Finlator. He, more than anyone else I'd met in my Angel Farm days, recognized and acknowledged that becoming and being a brown Angel was more than playing a lyre and singing celestial songs. Pain and pleasure and tears and treasures were part of the process and price, at least in my case. He and I both knew that my graduation was a victory not just for this brown Angel, but also for future Angels whose skin colors would be brown, black, and white and all the shades in between.

Holding my Meredith diploma tightly in my hands, I scanned the crowd for my parents. Come on, come on! It's time to celebrate, pack the car, and begin this Brown Angel's flight into the future…now.

Angel Years-Photographs

Freshman portrait, Meredith College

Franklin, Lena, Cam, spring of senior year

Lena Epps Brooker

Senior portrait, Meredith College

Graduation day, Meredith College

Betty Orr, Franklin, Cam, and Lena on graduation day

About the Author

Lena Epps Brooker was born in North Carolina when Jim Crow laws were prevalent. As an American Indian with Sappony, Cherokee, and Lumbee lineage, she faced racial discrimination throughout much of her life. Her childhood showed her the importance of raising awareness about American Indians, especially in her home state. She served on the boards of a number of cultural organizations and has won several awards for her work.

Brooker was the first American Indian graduate of Meredith College. She earned her bachelor's degree in elementary education, taught school, and went on to work for the North Carolina state government, including the North Carolina Commission of Indian Affairs, and public and private sector organizations. She also received certification as a lay minister from the United Methodist Church.

Brooker and her husband, Jim, live near Asheville, North Carolina, with their dog, Mercy. They enjoy spending time with their daughters, Lora and Lindsey, and their families.

Author Photo by Laura Ayres

CPSIA information can be obtained
at www.ICGtesting.com
Printed in the USA
LVHW051820070723
751646LV00005B/290